Counseling Kids
with
Emotional and Behavioral Problems in the Schools

Mary N. Cook, MD   Kathy Weldon, MA

LOVE PUBLISHING COMPANY®
Denver • London • Sydney

 Published by Love Publishing Company
P.O. Box 22353
Denver, Colorado 80222
www.lovepublishing.com

Library of Congress Control Number: 2005921908

Copyright © 2006 by Love Publishing Company
Printed in the United States of America
ISBN 0-89108-313-8

Contents

Preface

When children experience emotional or behavioral problems in school, school counselors are typically the first line of defense. Teachers and parents frequently bring initial concerns about students to counselors. The task of screening for emotional problems and assessing the need for a referral to a pediatric mental health provider often rests with counselors. In general, a safe rule of thumb, when in question, is to make a referral.

A significant body of research demonstrates that anxiety and depressive disorders in children, especially, are significantly under-recognized and undertreated. In the Report of the Surgeon General's Conference on Children's Mental Health, the U.S. Public Health Service (2000) estimated that 1 in 10 children and adolescents suffer from a mental illness severe enough to cause some level of impairment. But, in any given year, only 1 in 5 of these affected youth receives specialty mental health services. Because most children attend school, there is ripe opportunity for early identification, referral, and intervention with children at risk.

We collaborated for three years in a school setting to assist children with emotional and behavioral problems. We allied with a number of school counselors, who were frequently tapped to work with children who were struggling emotionally or behaviorally. Children who go on to qualify for special education on the basis of emotional impairment often require mental health specialty services outside of school, but nonetheless, school counselors often find themselves continuing to work with these kids and their families in the school setting. We found the school counselors devoted to the children and eager to assist, especially those with special needs, but many expressed feeling ill-equipped or at a loss for how to proceed. Some counselors said that they simply didn't know how or where to begin, and some doubted whether they were adequately qualified to intervene with emotionally disturbed children at all.

We developed a number of successful strategies for helping such children in the school setting and felt compelled to share them with school counselors in the form of this book. Most of the interventions are geared toward elementary school children, ages 5–12. The strategies apply to working with kids both individually and in groups and often require the participation and cooperation of parents, peers, teachers, and school administrators. These strategies are intended to serve as beginning building blocks for school counselors, upon which they can grow their own programs, based on their own context and experiences. They are not intended as a substitute for pediatric mental health services offered in a medical setting.

Each chapter provides a brief review of assessment techniques and epidemiology for the major types of disorders before covering suggestions for interventions. Also included are detailed appendixes of exercises, sample scripts, and behavioral contracts that school counselors may find useful in their continuing efforts to provide the best services possible. All can be photocopied for easy use, and some can be posted around a classroom or office as friendly reminders to children of new techniques they have learned.

Mary Cook, MD, is board-certified in child and adolescent psychiatry and general psychiatry and works at the Naval Medical Center in Portsmouth, Virginia.

Kathy Weldon, MA, is a school psychologist working for Department of Defense schools in Yokosuka, Japan.

The Depressed Child: What to Do With Kids Who Are Sad

by Mary Cook, MD

*A*child who is suspected of having clinical depression will likely need an evaluation and intervention by a credentialed pediatric mental health specialist. Still, school counselors often find themselves encountering children with depression. Sometimes school counselors are even required to meet on an ongoing basis with depressed children as part of an individualized education plan. In our experience, the level of comfort of counselors in intervening with emotionally disturbed children is variable. Some counselors feel ill equipped to work with these children at all and may not have had much training or experience in this area. As much as they would like to help, they often don't know what to do.

EPIDEMIOLOGY AND MAJOR FEATURES

Depression rates in children have been reported as high as 2.5% in children and 8% in adolescents (Birmaher, Ryan, Williamson, Brent, & Kaufman, 1996a). In children, boys are affected at the same rate as girls, whereas in adolescence, the ratio of girls to boys rises to 2:1. There are some developmental differences in the way depression presents in children. Separation anxiety, behavioral problems, somatic complaints, and phobias tend to accompany depression in children. Other symptoms of depression that tend to manifest in youth, particularly in adolescence, include feeling unloved, self-deprecation, disobedience, and angry outbursts. Children often don't have the classic depressive symptoms exhibited in adult depression, such as anhedonia, or the inability to experience pleasure, and disturbed sleep and appetite. Adults and youth both are likely to experience tearfulness, impaired concentration, hopelessness, suicidal thoughts, social isolation, and impaired functioning as part of their depression. Most youth, between 40% and 70%, have psychiatric disorders in addition to their depression, such as anxiety disorders, disruptive behavior disorders, and substance abuse. Depression tends to run in families, with children of depressed parents three times more likely to have an episode of depression.

ASSESSMENT

Assessing for depression in youth can be a bit like veterinary medicine. Children who are depressed aren't likely to say that they are depressed or even sad. Children, especially those 12 and under, are generally pretty unsophisticated in terms of understanding their own emotions and psychology. Instead, depression in childhood is more likely to show up as irritability, acting out or disruptive behavior, social withdrawal, or perhaps a deterioration in grades. It is likely that a deterioration in behavior or academic performance may be linked to environmental stressors as well, acute or chronic, such as academic failure, rejection by peers, or separations from caregivers.

In assessing for possible depression, it may be useful to interview the child, his teachers, and his parents. Sometimes classroom or playground observations are helpful. In conducting interviews, it is important to use open-ended questions and avoid leading or close-ended questions. For instance, beginning a question with, "Tell me about _____ (school, your family, soccer)" works better and yields significantly greater and more reliable information than, "Are you depressed?" or "Do you dislike school?"

To help in determining the severity of a possible depression and the need for referral to specialty services, it may be prudent to perform a standardized depression screening inventory such as the Children's Depression Inventory (Kovacs, 1985) or the Reynolds Adolescent Depression Scale (Reynolds & Richmond, 1978). These instruments are quick and easy to administer, require no special training, and are available commercially.

INTERVENTIONS

Empathy

School counselors can offer something very valuable to children with emotional problems. It is free and easy to provide. It's called empathy. Empathy offered by a caring, interested adult can be a very powerful cathartic to a child who is experiencing strong, especially negative, feelings. We all would like someone to listen to us and understand and validate our feelings, especially when we are upset. This may seem simplistic and obvious, but it is not the approach that many adults take when faced with a child expressing strong, negative feelings such as anger or sadness. Most adults find it difficult to tolerate witnessing the expression of strong anger or sadness by children. We want them to stop emoting and feel better now! Our first impulse may be to dismiss their feelings: "It's really not that bad." This approach is not usually helpful, though, because the feelings being expressed are real and often intense to children, whether or not we adults think there is a valid reason for feeling them.

It's helpful to remember that what upsets one person doesn't necessarily upset another. News that is devastating to a 9-year-old girl may not be earth-shattering to a 40-year-old man. The idea is not necessarily to agree with the child that whatever happened would be terrible and upsetting to anyone, but just that the counselor understands that the child feels terrible and is upset. The counselor can also communicate that she knows what it is like to be upset, sad, angry, or frustrated because all humans have experienced the same range of emotions at one time or other, albeit for different reasons. Empathy consists of two elements: first, identifying the feeling in another person, and second, conveying to that person that you understand the expressed feelings. It is helpful to use a specific feeling word, not to simply say "I understand how you feel." It is sometimes therapeutic to express to children that you *wish* you could give them what they want. You can join children in expressing and elaborating upon their fantasies, about what they wish would happen. Or, you can simply point out what it is that you think they want. Some sample effective empathic statements include:

- "Gosh, it sounds like you really, really wanted to make the cheerleading squad. I wish you had! In fact, I wish you could be the captain of the squad!!"
- "Boy, you sound pretty mad. It sounds like you wish you could get back at him."
- "You really look upset. I bet you really had your heart set on acing that test."
- "You sure seem frustrated about that. You really expected to make the team."

What if you guess wrong in trying to identify children's feelings or fantasies? No harm done. Children will let you know immediately. "No, I'm not sad, I'm mad!" You can encourage them to help you understand their feelings and predicament. They will usually be anxious to set you straight and make you see their point of view.

In addition to dismissing feelings as being invalid ("It's ridiculous to be upset about that!"), the other common, unhelpful, initial reaction of adults to an upset child is a rush to "solve the problem" or give advice. Problem solving is a useful skill to teach children, but the timing must be right. When children are in the midst of intense feelings, they first need an opportunity to emote, process their feelings, and have their feelings validated. When they are ready, they can be assisted to problem solve. Giving advice is almost never helpful or welcomed. What kids want and need in the midst of an upset moment is someone with whom to process their feelings. They will usually reject advice. Besides, giving advice and trying to solve their problems for them denies children the opportunity to work through and solve problems on their own.

Consider the following example:

Sally was a 9-year-old girl with depression, anxiety, and peer relational problems, who spilled water on her pants during a group therapy session at school. She was extremely sensitive to rejection and felt mortified by this experience. She immediately exited the group and was adamant that she could never face this group of peers again. Her thoughts were, "They think I'm clumsy, stupid, and babyish." Her father learned about this and reacted by dismissing her feelings. "No one cares about you spilling water on your pants! You're overreacting!" The problem is that when someone dismisses children's feelings as invalid, they feel ashamed and belittled. They become more upset and often try hard to convince others that they had good reason to react as they did. Dismissing a child's feelings as being inappropriate or exaggerated is not helpful.

Instead, consider empathy. A dialog with Sally that would be helpful and therapeutic to her might go as follows:

Counselor: "You look as though you feel embarrassed."

Sally: "I am. I'm mortified! I can never show my face again!"

Counselor: "Hmmm. Tell me more about that."

Sally: "Well, I'm younger than the other kids and they probably all think I'm a clumsy baby."

Counselor: "It must feel awful to think that."

Sally: "Yes! I feel humiliated!"

Counselor: "I know what that feels like. I have felt embarrassed in the past too."

*Sally: "Really?" (Sniffs, wipes away tears and looks up with interest.)
"When were you embarrassed?"*

*Counselor: "Well, this one time I spilled spaghetti on my white shirt in
the middle of a luncheon with my boss. I was sooooo embarrassed..."*

Sally and the counselor laugh.

Supportive Counseling

Supportive counseling is really just active listening with an attempt to
bolster the child's already existing psychological defenses. The counselor presents herself as a safe, nonjudgmental adult who holds the
child's very best interests at heart. Some children with emotional problems may not have a safe, nonjudgmental adult stashed at home or any-
place else. Sometimes a counselor can fill that role, perhaps providing
an "auxiliary superego" to children who are a little behind in developing their own. Child psychoanalysts believe that an adult, usually a
therapist, who follows a child long-term, can heal a child psychologically by providing a "corrective emotional experience." This refers to
the notion that an adult can help children accept and love themselves by
showing them "unconditional positive regard," which essentially means
that the adult is consistently warm, accepting, and supportive toward
them, regardless of what they say, do, or think. Bowlby (1979) captured
the essence of what it means to feel as though another human being is
consistently available and supportive of you:

*Evidence is accumulating that human beings of all ages are happi-
est and able to deploy their talents to best advantage when they
are confident that, standing behind them, there are one or more
trusted persons who will come to their aid should difficulties arise.
The person trusted, also known as an attachment figure, can be
considered as providing his (or her) companion with a secure base
from which to operate. (p. 103)*

It is helpful if the counselor makes every effort to communicate that
he or she appreciates the child's viewpoint and is interested in what the
child thinks and feels. The counselor might do best to simply listen to
what the child is saying and demonstrate attention by echoing back or
paraphrasing what has been said.

If the counselor is meeting with a child to provide counseling, it is essential to protect the therapeutic environment by ensuring that there are no interruptions or distractions. Any cell phone, beeper, or the ringer on the phone should be turned off. The door should be closed and display a "Do Not Interrupt" sign. Children need to feel as if they are important and their time with the counselor is protected and a priority for the counselor. They want undivided attention. Counselors, simply by actively listening and expressing empathy, can help children process feelings and arrive at workable solutions. Counselors can offer children unconditional positive regard. They can be safe people with whom children won't feel judged or criticized. The idea is to convey the sense, "I'm okay with who you are, no matter what." This helps children be okay with themselves, no matter what.

A great way to build rapport with a child, especially one who has been facing lots of failure and negative feedback from the environment, is to focus initially on areas of strength, on "islands of competence," to use a term coined by Sam Goldstein, MD. It may be difficult in some cases to uncover a child's strengths, but it will likely lead to the child sharing extensively and spontaneously. If children are given the opportunity to highlight their special talents and interests, rapport with them will be forthcoming. They will feel as though you view them in a positive light and that you are on their side. Plus, they will have much to share in regard to a realm where they can present themselves as experts or at least as passionate fans.

Problem Solving

When the child is ready to problem solve, the counselor's role should be to guide and support but *not direct.* Authors of effective parenting programs such as Brooks and Goldstein (2001) and Faber and Mazlish (1980) point out the importance of fostering a climate that encourages children to become independent thinkers. In *The Explosive Child,* Greene (2001) points to deficits in problem-solving skills as well as affect regulation as fundamental roots for explosive behavior.

The idea is to help children become adept at solving their own problems and for these skills to become second nature. The ultimate goal is for children to make good choices whether you are in the room or not. The steps of problem solving, easily remembered with the pneumonic D.I.R.T., are detailed in Chapter 7, "The Disruptive or ADHD Child," and will not be repeated here. A sample problem-solving scenario might go like this:

Ben: "I'm so mad. I could just kill Tom. He borrowed my bike and brought it back broken!"

Counselor: "Boy, you sound really angry. You really wish you could get him back for the way he hurt you." (Use of empathy, diffusion of strong negative affect)

Ben: "Yeah. I'd really like to break his favorite toy."

Counselor: "Yeah, I bet you wish you could smash his new computer game!" (Reflective listening, empathy)

Ben: "Yeah!! I'd like to wreck every one of his toys! Then he'd know how I feel!"

Counselor: "You'd really like for him to know how upset you are."

Ben: "That's right. I want him to pay for what he did."

Counselor: "Hmmm. I can see that you want something done about this broken bike of yours. Can you think of some ways to approach this problem?" (Encouraging brainstorming)

With some encouragement, Ben might generate a list like this:

I could punch Tom's lights out.

I could break one of his toys.

I could tell him how I feel.*

I could forget about the whole thing and fix the bike all by myself.

I could ask him to help pay for the repairs.*

I could end our friendship and never speak to him again.

I could tell his mom.

Hopefully, during the assessment stage, Ben will conclude that the best outcomes are likely to occur if he chooses the two options marked with an *. The other options will lead to tension or a termination of their friendship. Not holding Tom accountable for his actions is not an acceptable option, because it is a passive response and will cause Ben to feel resentful and bitter and powerless. Standing up to Tom in the right way, firmly and politely letting him know how Ben feels and asking him to assist with repairs, is likely to work best. With problems involving social conflict such as this, it's helpful to role play with the child and troubleshoot possible pitfalls to any given approach, in advance. Sample scenarios can be found in Chapter 3, in Table 3.1 on page 32.

The Unsafe Child: What to Do With Kids Who Threaten to Harm Themselves or Others

by Mary Cook, MD

*S*uicidal behavior is of great concern to clinicians and school personnel who deal with children with mental health problems. School counselors are not credentialed pediatric mental health specialists and cannot be expected to perform a psychiatric interview or determine safety risk for a child who verbalizes unsafe thoughts. Still, in the authors' experience, children with suicidal or homicidal thoughts often do first present to the school counselor. For most schools, the standard protocol when a child presents with safety concerns is to call an ambulance or escort the child to the nearest emergency room.

EPIDEMIOLOGY AND MAJOR CHARACTERISTICS

Suicide is exceedingly rare before puberty. The incidence of suicide attempts reaches a peak during mid-adolescence and in fact suicide becomes the third leading cause of death during the late teens (Schaffer & Pfeffer, 2001). Approximately 2,000 U.S. adolescents commit suicide each year. It is estimated that each year in the U.S., about 7 million adolescents attempt suicide and almost 700,000 receive medical attention for their attempt. In 1997, the mortality rate from suicide was 1.6 per 100,000 for 10- to 14-year-olds and 9.5 per 100,000 for the 15- to 19-year-old. The suicide rate for the older group was significantly higher in boys at a relative rate of 15.2 per 100,000 verses 3.4 per 100,000 in girls. Put another way, the ratio of completed suicides in adolescent males verses females is 5.5:1. Suicide attempts, on the other hand, are more common in girls than boys with ratio of 1.6:1.

Nearly all the adolescents (more than 90%) who commit suicide suffer from a psychiatric disorder at their time of death. More than half of them have suffered from psychiatric illness for at least two years prior to suicide. Situational stressors that are often associated with an adolescent suicide include loss of a romantic relationship, disciplinary, legal, or academic problems, and family conflict. Other risk factors include mood, disruptive behavior and substance abuse disorders, poor parent-child communication, and past suicidal behavior. Still, only half of all suicide completers have made a known serious attempt before their death. Family psychopathology and suicidal behavior also pose an increased risk. Gay, lesbian, and bisexual youth are at increased risk for suicide, often having multiple risk factors. So are adolescents who've been victims of sexual abuse.

There are ethnic differences in adolescent suicide rates with Caucasians having higher rates than African Americans. Native American and Alaskan Native youth have very high rates of suicide and Hispanic youth attempt suicide at higher rates than African American or Caucasian children.

RISK ASSESSMENTS

In assessing a suicidal patient it is essential to examine for any of the aforementioned risk factors. It is important to obtain information from multiple sources (school staff, peers, parents) and evaluate for the presence of suicide intent (a true wish to die), a plan, the lethality of that plan, any previous attempts, and access to means to execute the plan.

Sometimes counselors are unclear whether or not they have a suicidal or homicidal child on their hands. Sometimes kids get referred to see the counselor because of a morbid poem, song, or piece of art they created. If there is any doubt in regard to a child's safety, the recommendation is to be conservative and err on the side of caution. An unscheduled visit to the emergency room might be inconvenient and embarrassing for a child and his or her parents, but the alternative, should serious risk of harm be overlooked, is worse.

The following are some questions the counselor can ask to garner some relevant information regarding suicidality:

- *Tell me in your own words what you said or did leading to your referral to me?*
- *Did you ever hurt yourself on purpose?*
- *Have you had thoughts before of wanting to hurt yourself?*
- *Were you really feeling as though you wanted to die at the time you had these thoughts?*
- *Did you think of a way you might hurt yourself?*

The three most serious risk factors for suicide in a youth are a history of past suicide attempts, psychiatric illness, and substance abuse.

Similar questions and risk factors are important in assessing homicidality or violence. Does the child have intent or a strong wish to harm others? A plan? Means to carry out the plan? Psychiatric illness or a substance abuse problem? The most predictive risk factor for violence is a history of past violence. Additional risk factors for homicidality or violence are the presence of conduct disorder, a neuropsychological impairment, or an intellectual deficit. Children who have a history of preoccupation with morbid themes and death are thought to be at higher risk, as are children who lack a healthy peer group and complain of loneliness and rejection by peers.

INTERVENTIONS

Most of the research regarding public health measures aimed at preventing adolescent suicide have yielded discouraging results. Study of the effectiveness of crisis hotlines, public health measures restricting firearms, and school-based suicide awareness programs have not demonstrated significant reductions in rates of suicide in youth. What appears to be more effective in reducing suicide rates are programs designed to screen for associated mental illness, particularly depression.

Consider the following example:

Jerome was a fifth-grade student who had demonstrated adjustment problems since the first day of school. Although initially he was a disruptive student in the classroom, over a period of months his behavior improved considerably. However, he often seemed morose and unhappy. Fortunately, he had developed a good and trusting relationship with his teacher—so much so, in fact, that one day he completed an assignment by writing an essay (creatively utilizing his spelling words), in which he described his intent to commit suicide.

Jerome's spelling assignment, which he eagerly presented to his teacher, was clearly a "cry for help" to someone whom he had begun to believe really cared about him. His teacher immediately responded by sending him directly to Kathy, the school psychologist.

Her interview, which led to his immediate referral for medical intervention, went something like this:

Kathy (after reading aloud his essay): Jerome, these are some very distressing things you have written about. Does your essay represent your real feelings?

Jerome: Yes, I'm mad and I'm going to kill myself so that everyone will know how mad I am.

Kathy: From reading your words I can clearly see that you are very upset. How long have you been feeling this way?

Jerome: For a long time.

Kathy: Can you think of a time when you first started thinking about killing yourself?

Jerome: I tried to kill myself before.

Kathy: When was that? About how long ago?

Jerome: Maybe a month ago.

Kathy: How did you try to kill yourself?

Jerome: I tried hanging myself in my closet but it just broke.

Kathy: Sounds like you were really wanting to die but it didn't happen at that time. Did anyone know that you tried to kill yourself?

Jerome: My sister knew 'cause she came in and saw me and she told mom.

Kathy: And what happened after that?

Jerome: My sister started crying and my mom got angry and told me I was acting like a fool.

Kathy: But it sounds to me as though you haven't changed your mind about wanting to kill yourself. From your essay and what you are telling me, you are still very determined to die.

Jerome: Yeah, I'm going to do it to show them.

Kathy: Who do you want to show?

Jerome: Everybody—my mom, dad, sisters. They don't believe me. They don't care.

(By this time of course, Kathy had clearly established the need for a referral. Jerome had already made one attempt. He clearly articulated his determination to, and reasoning for, committing suicide. Kathy continued the interview with the following questions to explore the imminence of Jerome's intentions. Did Jerome have an immediate and viable plan to commit suicide?)

Kathy: How are you thinking you will kill yourself, Jerome? Would you try hanging yourself again?

Jerome: No, I'm going to jump from my apartment building. I live on the sixth floor.

Kathy: And when, Jerome, are you thinking you would do it? Have you thought about a time or day?

Jerome: I'm going to do it on my sister's birthday, February 4. That way her birthday will be ruined forever.

Having established a viable plan (jumping from a fatal height is one of the preferred methods of elementary-age children) and date (February 4 was less than one week away), Kathy recognized the need for an emergency intervention.

Kathy: I am very saddened that your life feels so bad that you would want to end it. People in your life need to know how badly you are feeling, and we need to do something to change your feelings. I need to tell your parents, and maybe they can get you to talk to a doctor or someone who can help you feel better.

Jerome: I won't talk to nobody. Don't tell anybody because then they'll try to stop me.

Kathy: You're right, Jerome, people will try to stop you from killing yourself because they care. I want to stop you.

Jerome: Well I'll just do it now, 'cause no one is going to stop me.

At this point Jerome jumped to his feet looking as though he intended to run out of the room and kill himself at that moment. Knowing the situation was urgent, Kathy slowly calmed him down.

Kathy: Jerome, I want to talk to you some more; please don't leave. Your feelings are very important to me. I can see how angry and upset you are. It sounds as though a whole lot of people have made you mad. I want to know more. Please sit down and let's talk some more.

Because the situation was clearly urgent and because of her fear that Jerome would act rashly to avoid having his plan thwarted, Kathy took great care in comforting and calming him and organizing an immediate intervention. After Jerome returned to his seat and again engaged in conversation, Kathy asked Jerome if she could make a phone call to the school counselor, Stacy, so that she could hear how upset Jerome was feeling. After another brief interview, Kathy and Stacy were able to persuade Jerome to accompany them to the school principal's office, stressing to him the importance of telling the principal how he was feeling. At some point, Kathy was able to leave Jerome and contact his parents and an emergency vehicle. Because Jerome protested and repeatedly threatened that no one would be able to stop him from killing himself, it ultimately required uniformed police officers to persuade Jerome to accompany them to a hospital emergency room where he was immediately hospitalized and later admitted to an extended residential treatment program.

Although Jerome's case was atypically urgent, all suicidal threats should be taken seriously. Counselors sometimes feel uncomfortable talking with a student about suicidal plans. Some have said that it somehow feels inappropriate to directly confront a student about plans to kill him/herself. The problem, however, is that the "threat," whether real or unlikely, is inevitably a cry for attention and help. In terms of demonstrating a caring attitude and deep commitment to the child's safety and well being, the more attention the student receives, the better. It is prudent to always respond strongly and immediately to any suicidal ideation. It's unproductive and perhaps unsafe to dance around the question of suicide with a student. It's essential to always inform the student's parents and make a follow-up referral.

The Socially Impaired Child: What to Do With Kids Who Can't Get Along With Others

—by Mary Cook, MD

*M*ost kids seem to acquire social skills naturally, for the most part, although many social skills are probably taught or modeled by parents, siblings, peers, and others. Most kids seem to sense intuitively how close is too close, how rough is too rough, when is the best time to join in or start a conversation. They can sense how others feel and respond appropriately and sensitively. Basic social skills are essential to help children get along in the world.

If you ask kids whether they like school or what they like best about school, a distinctive pattern emerges. Children who are well liked and have adequate friends, generally like or even love school, regardless of academic standing. Further, what they will tell you is that their favorite part of school is "chasing the boys," or "playing with Courtney (their best friend)." Rarely do children answer that what they like best about school is science or learning. If they did give such an answer, most of us would suspect they're being phony and acting in an Eddie Haskell kind of way.

On the other hand, kids who struggle socially generally hate school. They often do everything in their power to avoid attending school, such as throwing tantrums or feigning sick or even ditching classes. They will tell you that they hate school because no one likes them and they have no friends. Once again, you will rarely hear mention of academic struggles as the most prominent aversion to school, although many socially impaired children also struggle academically.

We all know kids who just don't get it. They play too rough, their sense of humor needs an explanation, and they constantly offend and annoy others. Children with disruptive behavior disorders are often socially impaired and struggle to make friends. So, too, by definition, children with autistic spectrum disorders, including Asperger's syndrome, suffer significant social deficits. They simply don't know how to read body language and other social cues. They can't accurately detect feelings in others and don't know how to make or keep friends. They struggle with even simple things such as making eye contact and introducing themselves.

What to do? Most socially impaired kids can be intellectually *taught* some basic social skills that others come by intuitively or naturally. Social skills training can occur individually, but ideally is delivered in a group setting, where children might have an opportunity to practice with peers and therefore learn *experientially* by role-playing and practicing their newfound skills. Groups for social skills training might strategically include at least a few model citizens who are particularly socially graced and well liked by peers, who can model adept social skills. The following strategies are offered as a starting point and are best delivered in the setting of a small group of 6–8 children who are similar in developmental level (say kids from grades 3–5).

INTERVENTIONS

Social Skills Training

Introducing Yourself

Children who are socially impaired often struggle to even get past the first step of making a friend, introducing themselves. They often come across as intrusive and offend others right off the bat. However, the art of social introductions can be taught and, with a little practice, can be mastered.

An important point to convey to kids regarding delivering the right kind of introduction is to choose the right person at the right time. Timing is key. For example, kids need to be taught to wait for a lull in the conversation if they want to introduce themselves to peers who are talking. Also, they need to be taught about personal space. Many socially inept kids are intrusive—they crowd others and say offensive things. They are anxious to be noticed and often know only negative ways of garnering attention. They should be taught to make good and consistent eye contact, to stand an adequate distance away (an arm's length), face the other child directly, and shake hands in a congenial way. The handshake should be firm but not crushing, brief, and use the whole hand. Children younger than 12 do not customarily shake hands when greeting one another, but it is still worthwhile to introduce the concept of what is considered an ideal handshake. A useful analogy is to have them imagine they are applying for a job, meeting their potential boss, and want to make a good impression. Also, they need to be encouraged to smile. Everyone enjoys being smiled at, and if we are meeting someone who doesn't smile, we might feel rejected or assume the new person is grouchy or unfriendly. The goal is to convey a sense of warmth, friendliness, and confidence.

Making Conversation

Kids with social deficits aren't the best conversationalists. They might be too domineering during a dialogue or just can't seem to keep it going. They don't track conversations well and might respond in an odd or even offensive fashion. Sometimes, they just can't seem to figure out what to say.

The important points here are again timing, maintaining eye contact, smiling, and behaving in a friendly way. You can point out that everyone likes to talk and appreciates being listened to. You can suggest the best way to maintain a conversation is to ask questions—the right kind of questions. The right kind of questions are open-ended. For example, saying to someone, "Tell me about your _____ (family, house, hobby, dog, trip)" leaves lots of room for an expansive response. Follow-up responses such as "Tell me more about . . ." are helpful, asking for more details. Closed-ended questions produce one-word answers and are conversation killers. For example, "What's your favorite color?" is sure to get a one-word response. Conversation over. Trying to find a particular interest or hobby of the other child or some common ground is helpful, and showing interest in what the other child says through reflective listening keeps things going.

A fun and easy activity for practicing these skills involves creating a talk show. Have the kids come up with a name and arm yourself with a video camera. There's nothing kids love more than hamming it up in front of a video camera. A suggestion is to spend one session videotaping the kids pretending they are talk show hosts and the next session they can have a party and view the videos while munching pizza or popcorn or other treats.

You can first talk about how talk show hosts make their guests comfortable. They say nice things about them, greet them warmly with a firm handshake, and invite them to sit down. They often offer them something to drink and laugh at their guests' jokes, even when they're not funny. Good talk show hosts are friendly, complimentary, and good conversationalists. They ask lots of open-ended questions and follow-up questions and listen well. You and another group facilitator can demonstrate what you mean before inviting the kids to partner up and take turns pretending to run talk shows.

Listening Skills

Kids with social problems are often lousy listeners and this behavior alienates others. The tricks for being a good listener include maintaining eye contact, for starters. Many children fail to make eye contact spontaneously or are simply uncomfortable doing so. They must be encouraged to make it a habit and often require modeling and frequent reminders from adults. The goal is to make eye contact second nature for them and this can take some practice, time, and persistence.

It also helps kids if they learn to use reflective listening, where they repeat back parts of what others say or paraphrase what has been said. This technique is great for keeping conversations going and building relationships with others. Reflective listening demonstrates that you are interested in the other person and are tracking what he or she is saying. The sentence spoken by one child can be repeated by the other child, in the form of a question. For example, if Susie says, "I want you to draw a pink circle with polka dots," Johnnie could respond, "You want me to draw a pink circle with polka dots?" It helps to demonstrate good listening if the listening child responds relevantly to the speaking child, or expands on what has been said. For example, if Susie says, "I just moved here from Baltimore," Johnnie could say, "Oh, my grandmother lives in Baltimore. Tell me about it." Kids can also be coached to use body language to show they're listening. For example, they can show they're interested by leaning in and facing the other child directly.

Here's a list of examples of how children can demonstrate that they are being good listeners (also found on page 132 in Appendix A):

How to Show You Are Being a Good Listener

1. *Make eye contact.*
2. *Put down anything you're doing or looking at.*
3. *Don't talk while the other person is talking.*
4. *Respond to what the speaker says (e.g., answer a question).*
5. *Ask a relevant question or make a relevant comment.*
6. *Repeat back parts of what the speaker says.*
7. *Paraphrase what the speaker says.*

Giving Compliments

Socially impaired children often offend and annoy others. They may not realize it, but they say things that make others feel badly and put down. Sometimes, the kids are boastful and unduly focused on themselves. You can help them attract others by teaching them how to give good compliments. You can point out to them that everyone likes compliments. You can ask children how they feel when they are complimented. The key with giving an effective and appreciated compliment is to be specific. Not to say, "Oh, you're so wonderful," but something specific like, "I appreciate your honesty." Not to say, "What a great picture," but instead, "I love the bright colors in the rainbow and the detailed dog, which looks so real." It's important not to overdo. If you say, "Wow, that's the best drawing I've ever seen!" you will not appear sincere and your compliment will not mean much. Instead, be real, be specific, and compliment often. Compliments make us feel good, and we like to have friends who compliment and appreciate us.

Developing Empathy

Empathy involves viewing a situation from someone else's vantage point, particularly in reference to how one might be feeling. However, socially impaired children are typically inept at taking another's perspective and interpreting feelings accurately.

The capacity for experiencing and expressing empathy may be the most important skill in relationships. Brooks and Goldstein (2001) cite parental modeling and teaching of empathy as a key ingredient in fostering strong parent-child relationships and bolstering *resiliency,* the capacity to rebound from stress, in children. Regular expression of empathy can go a long way toward building and maintaining strong relationships and buffering children from stress. Many adults struggle to master this skill and may not actively demonstrate empathy to their children. But to be successful socially, kids must regularly employ empathy. You can introduce the concept by asking whether feelings are important. Everyone will agree they are. Children can be asked whether they think their feelings are important and whether or not they want their feelings to be understood by others and taken seriously. Everyone will agree on these points, too. We all think our feelings are important, and we all want others to understand our feelings and treat them as though important.

There are two basic components to empathy: 1) understanding another's feelings, and 2) conveying to another that you understand those feelings.

You can ask for ideas regarding how we know what others are feeling. The answer is facial expression, body language, tone of voice, and content of what is said. Sometimes others will tell you what they are feeling, but it's important to point out that many times kids keep their feelings inside and won't spontaneously express them directly and openly. Some children aren't very adept at identifying even their own feelings and might act them out instead. Ask kids whether they recall being upset and whether they found it helpful to talk about their feelings to a friend, parent, or teacher.

Programs for children by Shapiro (1994), Kendall (2000), and others highlight the importance of promoting a so-called feelings vocabulary in children, especially in those children who demonstrate emotional and behavioral problems. A fun and handy way to approach this is to have small groups of children perform miming exercises that use cards with various feeling words—the more the better, including basic feeling words such as sad, mad, and glad, but also more sophisticated words such as disappointed, frustrated, and thoughtful (see Figure 3.1; these cards can also be found on page 133 in Appendix A and can be laminated and cut out for repeated use). Kids can be handed cards and asked to act out their feelings while others guess, kind of like charades. Points, stickers, or tokens can be awarded for correct guesses and later traded in for prizes. The group can be partnered up and kids can practice making statements of empathy such as, "You seem sad" or "You look frustrated." Those simple statements can be very comforting to

SAD	EXCITED	ECSTATIC
MAD	HAPPY	FURIOUS
DREAMY	DISAPPOINTED	TERRIFIED
HOPEFUL	FRUSTRATED	WORRIED
SCARED	EMBARRASSED	UPSET
IN LOVE	THOUGHTFUL	CONFUSED

FIGURE 3.1   FEELINGS VOCABULARY

others and open up conversations where a child can express his feelings and garner support from a peer. You can point out that empathy statements convey that you care about that other person and can also serve as an invitation to talk about feelings further. In addition, most people appreciate a chance to talk about their feelings when they're upset.

Comforting an Upset Friend

Many people (especially socially inept children) feel awkward and at a loss when faced with needing to comfort a friend who is upset. People commonly take a number of approaches in an effort to quickly defuse the upset being experienced by another person. We don't like seeing others upset and many people, both adults and children, tend to attempt to minimize the reason for the upset or attempt to solve the problem for their friends. Usually these efforts are well intended, but typically do little to comfort friends in need, as they tend to feel as though their feelings or problems are being minimized or dismissed. If people perceive that their feelings are not understood or are dismissed as invalid, they will typically work hard to convince others that they do in fact have good reason to be upset. In the process, they tend to become more upset. In the book *How to Talk So Kids Will Listen and Listen So Kids Will Talk,* Faber and Mazlish (1980) outline some common mistakes parents make in responding to their children when they are upset. Similar errors are made in all types of relationships, as most people, both adults and children, simply have never learned good ways of comforting a friend in need. A few common errors, as well as some helpful approaches to comforting an upset friend, follow (these can also be found on page 134–135 in Appendix A).

Things That *Don't* Help a Friend Who's Upset

Vague Response

"I understand how you feel."

This response is not specific enough. If you say this, you may seem insincere or patronizing. Use a specific feeling word.

Invalidating Feelings

"That's no reason to be upset."

It is important to emphasize with kids that all feelings are important to the person experiencing them. You can ask them whether the same things that make them sad or angry make their brother or mother or teacher sad or angry. You can help them recognize that we all react differently to the same situation. What makes other children sad or angry might not affect them the same way. The point to remember is that we all have had the same feelings at one time or other. We all know what it is like to feel angry, sad, or disappointed. The message to share is that "I know what it's like to feel _____ (fill in the blank with a specific word)" or "I can see that you are feeling _____ (fill in)." Also, by conveying you understand their feelings and inviting them to talk, you are showing you think their feelings are important. This is a great gift to give a friend, and it's free.

Problem Solving

"It will be easy to fix your bike," or "Why don't you just buy another one?"

Many kids (and adults, for that matter) make this mistake when trying to comfort a friend. We think everything would be fine if we could just solve the problem. Problem solving is a useful skill, but the timing must be right. Initially, what is helpful when others are upset is simply expressing empathy, validating their feelings, and inviting them to talk about their feelings. Rushing to solve their problems often makes others feel as if their feelings are being dismissed or invalidated.

Giving Advice

"Why don't you just go tell the teacher you didn't cheat?"

Again, advice right off the bat is not usually helpful or welcomed by a friend who is hurting. Instead, wait for advice to be sought. In the meantime, express empathy and actively listen. Just be there.

Things That *Do* Help a Friend Who's Upset

Reflective Listening

As mentioned, reflective listening is simply repeating back part of what someone says or paraphrasing it. It is very therapeutic and makes others feel as though you care and are listening.

For example, a friend says, "I feel so terrible that I failed that test. I'm so afraid my mother will be furious."

You say, "You're scared you'll get in trouble with your mother for failing."

Empathy

This refers to trying to understand what someone is feeling and conveying it back to him or her.

For example, a friend is crying, so you say, "You seem upset."

Formulas for Expressing Empathy:

You sound _____ (fill in with feeling word).

You look _____ (fill in with feeling word).

I sense that you feel _____ (fill in with feeling word).

Collaborative Problem Solving

Greene (2001) has developed a program for explosive children built around an intervention he has termed *collaborative problem solving*. His program involves adults assisting children by essentially empowering them to solve their own problems. They do this by serving as a sounding board and providing some emotional support in the face of a crisis or conflict. This technique can also be a therapeutic intervention that friends use to support each other and can be taught to children 10 and over as an option for helping a friend in crisis. It is quite different than attempting to solve friends' problems for them when they are upset, which would likely leave them feeling inadequate and as if their feelings were dismissed. Consider the following example:

Your friend is upset because she might get cut from the school soccer team.

The friend says, "I'll just die if I don't make the team."

You say, "Hmmm . . . sounds like you'd be crushed if you didn't make the school team."

Your friend says, "Yeah, I just couldn't bear it."

You say "Hmmmm. I wonder what you could do if you didn't make the team."

Your friend says, "I'd just cry and cry."

You say, "Yeah, it would be sad. Do you think there are any other things you could do?"

Your friend says, "Well, I suppose I could go out for the soccer team at the YMCA. It is co-ed, and there are some cute boys who go there."

You say, "That sounds like fun!"

Just Being There/Just Listening

This is fairly self-explanatory. When people are upset, it is helpful just to be with them and listen if they want or need to talk. Having someone who cares about you standing by when you're upset is extremely healing. You don't have to say a word, *just be there.*

Using Conflict Resolution

Thomas Gordon, author of *Parent Effectiveness Training* (2000), suggests that effective conflict resolution is the most critical ingredient to any successful relationship. There are lots of ways to approach social conflict but few are ideal and result in a "win-win" resolution. Children with impaired social skills often struggle with resolving social conflict. They tend to use approaches that turn others off or that have negative consequences. You can aid them a great deal by teaching them the art of effective conflict resolution. The topic can be introduced to socially impaired kids by gently having them take note that their past approaches to social conflict were unsuccessful and only got them rejected or in trouble. You can engage their interest by sharing that there are ways of approaching conflicts that are actually relationship-building and increase the odds of them getting what they want.

Conflict resolution, just as with other types of social skills, is ideally taught in a group format. It is helpful to set up a group that consists partly of socially impaired children but also includes a few children who are socially gracious, to serve as peer role models. A first step could be to ask the children to define social conflict. After some discussion, you can offer an appropriate definition, such as: "A disagreement between two people when they have competing needs or wants." You might then ask, "What is a resolution?" An appropriate definition might be: "That's when two parties involved in a conflict arrive at a solution that meets both of their needs."

One of the most important lessons about social conflict is that it almost always develops secondary to miscommunication and misunderstanding. It is essential to understand this because it implies that most conflict can be resolved fairly simply via discussion and clarification. Also, as one party in a conflict begins to understand the other party's perspective and feelings, usually anger, resentment, and frustration fade away.

Ask the children in the group to think of examples of conflicts from their own lives or make up examples. Ask them to give specific examples of conflicts that resulted from miscommunication. You can mention rumors as an example of where untruths are spread, leading to hurt feelings and conflict.

It is also helpful to point out that many instances of conflict are due to circumstances or accidents. Have children give examples and discuss how circumstances out of our control can result in conflict between people. Examples include a traffic jam or accident causing someone to be late to meet a friend, or one friend making the soccer team but not the other.

Ask kids for their ideas for approaching a conflict. Have them brainstorm as you write their answers on the board. Encourage them to generate a lengthy list, accepting even strategies that don't work well. The list might look like this:

- I could punch his lights out.
- I could tell on him.
- We could compromise.
- I could give in.
- I could apologize.
- I could make a joke about it.
- We could get a mediator.

You can have the kids go through the list and cross off options that don't work well. You can have them offer their opinions regarding which answers are best and which options would cause further problems. The options that generally work best involve compromise, humor, an apology, mediation, assertiveness, ignoring or walking away, taking turns, or using chance, such as flipping a coin or drawing straws; these are listed on page 136 in Appendix A. Aggression, tattletaling, and giving in usually don't resolve the conflict well and end up with someone getting hurt or teased. Tattletales, especially in the school, can be mercilessly teased. Plus a tattletaler doesn't learn the art of resolving conflicts in an ideal way—on his own. However, if a child is being bullied excessively, adult intervention, even involvement of school administration or security, may be needed.

You can draw the following grid on a chalk or dry-erase board to show all possible results, using a different color to denote Johnnie and Susie. A plus sign indicates that one of them wins; a minus sign indicates that one loses.

	Johnnie wins (+)	Johnnie loses (−)
Susie loses (−)	− +	− −
Susie wins (+)	+ +	+ −

You can ask the kids which box represents the best outcome. They will tell you the best outcome is one where both parties win. Therefore, the goal of conflict resolution is to arrive at a compromise where both kids get something they want, although they might also have to give up something. You can have them generate scenarios (e.g., you and your brother both want to play video games at the same time, or your sister broke your new bike) and role-play efforts at conflict resolution. Some sample scenarios to help kids practice resolving conflicts appear in Table 3.1, as well as on page 137 in Appendix A.

Learning Assertiveness

Children need to learn how to stand up for themselves (with their words) and ask for what they want or need in the right way. Aggression and anxiety usually go hand in hand. Kids often behave verbally or physically aggressive when they feel threatened or hurt, or are afraid they won't get their needs met. Teaching them assertiveness gives them an ideal mechanism for expressing their needs and increases the likelihood they will get their needs met. You can begin by introducing the four styles of communication: passive, passive-aggressive, aggressive, and assertive. The types of communication can be defined as follows (these can also be found on page 138 in Appendix A):

- *Passive:* A passive style of communication implies saying or doing nothing when faced with a social conflict or distressing situation.

TABLE 3.1   SAMPLE SOCIAL CONFLICT SCENARIOS

Your best friend likes the same boy you do.	Your friend borrowed your bike and broke it.	Your mom said you have to clean your room, but your friends are waiting for you to play outside.
You caught your friend cheating on a test.	You have invitations to two birthday parties on the same day.	You want to play soccer, but your friend wants to play football.
One of your friends dislikes your other friend.	Your mom asks you why you failed a test.	You can't agree with your sister on what to watch on TV.
Your dad asks you about losing your new jacket.	Your classmate wants to copy your homework.	Your teacher accused you of doing something you didn't do.
Your sister won't stop singing.	Your friend lied to you.	The boy next to you won't stop talking in class.

- *Passive-Aggressive:* Passive-aggressive communication refers to a style whereby people display hostility or aggression in a covert way. For example, they might deliberately lose or forget something, or show up late to meet someone with whom they are angry.
- *Aggressive:* Aggressive communication refers to physical or verbal aggression, whereby overt hostility is expressed in a way intended to deliberately hurt others.
- *Assertive:* Assertive communication is considered the ideal style. It involves openly and honestly expressing one's feelings without using shame, blame, or put-downs and making simple and clear requests of others.

You can present some scenarios where an assertive response is appropriate and offer possible response choices that demonstrate all four communication styles, as in Figure 3.2, part of which is also found on pages 138 and 139 in Appendix A.

You are in a crowded movie theater and the guys behind you won't stop talking.

a. You ignore them. (Passive)
b. You politely ask them to stop talking so you can enjoy the movie. (Assertive)
c. You start talking loudly, too, to annoy them. (Passive-aggressive)
d. You throw your popcorn and drinks at them. (Aggressive)

You are in a restaurant and the waitress brings you the wrong order.

a. You eat what she brought you and say nothing. (Passive)
b. You call her "stupid" and start screaming. (Aggressive)
c. You pout in an obvious way but deny there is a problem when your mom asks if there's a problem. (Passive-aggressive)
d. You say, "Ma'am, this is not what I ordered. I had requested a hot dog, not pizza." (Assertive)

An additional exercise would be to have the children role-play various scenarios, such as the following:

1. The bike repair shop overcharged you $20 and did work you didn't request.
2. The cafeteria server gave you the wrong lunch.
3. Your sister won't stop teasing you about your freckles.
4. Your friend wants to borrow your new game, but you don't want him to.
5. A bully butted in line.
6. The teacher accuses you of cheating, but you didn't.
7. You want to play basketball, but your friend wants to play baseball.
8. Your friend wants to borrow your new toy, but you don't wish to share it.

FIGURE 3.2   FOUR STYLES OF COMMUNICATION

You can teach children that asserting yourself is about saying what's on your mind in a firm but polite way. The idea is to put other people in your shoes and help them understand your perspective and feelings, how you are being affected by their behavior. Encourage them to use "I" statements and express their feelings, but be careful not to attack the other person. Discourage them from name-calling or negatively labeling things or situations ("idiot," "inconsiderate," "loser," "useless," "worthless") because those approaches put the other person on the defensive or color a situation in an utterly negative light and subsequently tend not to lead to a positive conclusion. Instead, suggest they first say how they feel, point out the person's behavior they don't like (be specific), and make a request for a change.

Programs for assertiveness training, such as that by Hermes (1998), often advocate starting out with a handy formula for assertiveness such as the one that appears in Figure 3.3 and on page 140 in Appendix A. You can have kids practice and commit a similar formula to memory. As children master this style of communication, they can ad lib more and become less reliant on such formulas. Still, these are tough skills to master, even for adults, so expect this intervention to be fairly challenging (but not untenable).

An alternative to this formula is to become a "broken record." For instance, if Johnnie owes Susie $5, Johnnie may say, "But I don't

---

I FEEL _____ ("I" statement, identify and explain your feelings)

WHEN YOU _____ (Point out the behavior you don't like without insulting or attacking)

BECAUSE (optional) _____ (Help the other person understand your viewpoint, put him or her in your shoes)

I WOULD LIKE _____ (Make a request)

IN RETURN/THEN (optional) _____ (Let the other person know the positive consequences for both of you if he or she complies with your request)

FIGURE 3.3   ASSERTIVENESS FORMULA

have enough," to which Susie responds, "I'd like my $5 back." And on it goes with Susie repeating her request the same way, firmly but politely, over and over until Johnnie coughs up the $5 he owes her.

Joining In

Children with social skills deficits often don't know quite how to join a group. They can be like "bulls in a china shop," barging in when and where they are not wanted, or, due to a lack of confidence, stand back and go unnoticed, too reticent to join the fun. However, as with all social skills, the art of joining in can be taught.

The key to joining a game or other activity is timing. The idea is for kids to learn how to watch for an opportune time to join a group of peers at play. They can start by watching from the sidelines and perhaps wait for a lull in the game or for someone to get called out or call a time-out. Or they can wait for another child to voluntarily exit the game. Or they can stand by looking interested and hope to be invited to join in. Children must be cautioned to bear in mind that they are the "new guy" in these situations and to behave in the most polite and cooperative manner. They must be careful not to be too pushy or controlling if they are seeking entry into a group of peers at play.

A good analogy is the concept of interviewing for a job: You're trying to make a good impression on a group of peers you'd like to join. Sometimes, even when the timing and technique for joining in is right, a child may be consistently excluded. It's important to prepare kids for this inevitable event. They should be advised to expect to be turned down on occasion, but to keep trying. They can be asked to consider other explanations for why they were turned down, such as the other children perhaps being locked into a fierce competition. If a child is repeatedly turned down, you can set up exercises to actively role-play these attempts to join in and you and peers can troubleshoot for problems with the technique the child uses.

Hosting

Children who are socially impaired are not usually gracious hosts and hostesses. They tend to be controlling and insist that things go their way, even with guests in their homes. They may attempt to control the types of activities and snacks and disregard or simply fail to notice their guests' feelings and wishes. Kids with such deficits often either don't recognize body language and social nuances or they misread social cues. Either way, play dates with these children are recipes for disaster, at least without a little coaching.

There are a few things for kids and their parents to keep in mind when setting up play dates. Limiting to one guest works best. Two guests, which make a threesome when the host is added, is not a good idea. Three kids just don't play well together. Another basic rule of hospitality is that the guest is always right. Children should be taught to allow their guests to choose the first activity, to go first, and so on. It's important that kids be advised to prepare for their guest. They should look over their toys and belongings and be sure to stash away anything precious that they don't care to share. A brand new toy or newly built Lego tower should be safely stowed in a parent's closet before the guest arrives. That way, everything in view is up for grabs and the host will be comfortable sharing any possessions left out.

Handling Teasing

Many kids with social problems are the brunt of much teasing. Those children who don't get along well with peers usually have things about them that make them stand out in a negative way. They might look different (be overweight or have a facial deformity or skin condition), act different, talk funny (have articulation problems), or have learning or behavior problems. These kids need to be taught effective techniques for responding to teasing.

You can begin by asking them why kids tease. Facilitate a discussion that leads them to understand that children who tease want to elicit a strong emotional reaction from their victims. They like the thrill of pushing another child's emotional buttons. So you can help children recognize that a strong emotional reaction to teasing (lots of anger or tears) is very reinforcing to the teaser and is likely to result in more teasing. You can also point out that some kids tease because they feel badly about themselves and think that putting down others will help them feel better about themselves. Shapiro (1994) advises teaching children with anger problems some "tricks" for responding to teasing, so that they are prepared to use their words, not their fists. Some options include the following (a simplified version can be found on page 141 in Appendix A):

Tease Handles

Ignoring: This is the traditional advice given to kids by adults. It's not a bad technique and sometimes, eventually, results in an end to teasing. But many kids will tell you they can't stand to ignore the teasing or that ignoring doesn't work.

Fogging: This is a favored technique and usually eliminates teasing by leaving the teaser with nowhere to go. One method of so-called fogging is highlighted by Bourne (1995) in his work on assertive communication techniques for adults. Essentially, this technique involves agreeing with the teaser or even expanding on the tease. The idea is to show that the teasing isn't perturbing you in the least. This reaction is boring and not the desired result and usually results in the teaser giving up and moving on. A simple example of fogging is to simply have the child respond to an insult by saying "So what?!" or "Prove it!" Other examples appear below.

> Susie says, "You look scary and weird," to which Johnnie replies, "Thank you, I've been practicing."

> Johnnie says, "You're as fat as an elephant." Susie replies, "That's true, but could you be more specific—an African or an Asian elephant?"

Put Down the Tease: This is another clever and effective technique but takes some practice and rehearsal. It is important to distinguish between putting down the tease—which defuses the situation—versus putting down the teaser, which only escalates things. The idea is for the victim of teasing to convey to the teaser that the teasing is lame, isn't bothersome, and might as well be given up.

> Susie says, "You're so gay." Johnnie replies, "I've been hearing that since kindergarten!" (implying that the tease is old, unoriginal, and babyish).

> Johnnie says, "You are so fat." Susie replies, "Duh, I know! It's so obvious!"

With the techniques of fogging and putting down the tease, you tell children they don't really have to agree in their hearts with the teasing. You are just giving them a strategy to effectively put an end to the teasing. Fogging and putting down the tease catch the teaser off guard and usually render them speechless. Also, they are matter-of-fact, not highly emotional or dramatic, reactions, and the teaser usually finds this boring and moves on.

Broken Record: This is a simple but effective technique, which is mentioned as part of an anger management program for children by Shapiro (1994). You teach kids to respond to teasing with a simple phrase such as, "I don't like your teasing and I'm not going to say anything back." You advise them to try repeating this phrase, exactly the same way, in a matter-of-fact way, over and over when they encounter teasing. Eventually, most teasers give up and move on, because this reaction, too, is boring.

In most instances of teasing, these techniques will work and the child can learn to handle teasing on his or her own. However, there will be times that despite great efforts to abort the teasing, a child will fall victim to relentless and cruel teasing or bullying and adults need to intervene. Counselors can observe playground and classroom interventions and identify teasers and bullies and intervene with them, sometimes even involving school administrators and parents. Teasing can be very damaging and should be taken seriously.

The Anxious Child: What to Do With Kids Who Worry Too Much

by Mary Cook, MD

*A*child who is suspected of having clinically significant and impairing levels of anxiety is likely to need an evaluation and intervention by a credentialed pediatric mental health specialist. Still, school counselors often find themselves encountering children with anxiety. Sometimes school counselors are even required to meet on an ongoing basis with anxious children as part of an individualized education plan. Here are some basic strategies to assist school counselors in working with anxious or worrying children.

EPIDEMIOLOGY AND MAJOR CHARACTERISTICS

Epidemiological studies of school-aged children reveal the following rates for anxiety disorders: 3.5% for separation anxiety disorder, 2.9% for overanxious (now generalized anxiety) disorder, 2.4% for simple phobia, and 1.0% for social phobia (Bernstein, Borchardt, & Perwien, 1996). Prevalence rates for panic disorder are essentially unknown for children, although it appears that it is reportedly rare before puberty.

There are several studies pointing to a slow-to-warm-up temperament as being a risk factor for the development of an anxiety disorder. In particular, young children, ages 2–5, who are found to be behaviorally inhibited, shy, passive, or fearful are more likely to go on to develop an anxiety disorder. There are also family studies pointing to genetic factors as etiologic. For example, a study of children of parents with agoraphobia or obsessive-compulsive disorder revealed them to be at seven-fold greater risk of developing an anxiety disorder when compared to children of parents with no anxiety disorder. Insecure attachment in infancy has also been shown to predispose children to the development of anxiety.

Separation anxiety disorder is marked by clinically significant anxiety about separating from caregivers that is developmentally inappropriate. Generalized anxiety disorder criteria include excessive worry or anxiety about a variety of everyday situations, accompanied by one or more symptoms of physiological arousal (insomnia, muscle tension, impaired concentration). Specific or simple phobias are defined as excessive or unreasonable fears of circumscribed objects or situations where the distress related to the fear is functionally impairing. Social phobia is marked by undue excessive anxiety or distress associated with social situations in which the person is terrified of humiliation or rejection and functionally impaired by his or her symptoms. Panic disorder consists of recurrent panic attacks, which are periods of intense anxiety with physiological arousal. Also, the person has what is called anticipatory anxiety or fear of having future attacks.

ASSESSMENT

It's easy to miss an anxiety disorder in a child. Anxious children are often timid and inhibited and might go relatively unnoticed. Anxiety is a subjective, internal state, and cannot be observed easily except in instances where anxious children perceive threats and react in a defensive, hostile, or aggressive way. There are studies demonstrating that anxious children are less likely to act out, but a few studies have suggested just the opposite—that is, that anxious children are likely to behave aggressively. In my experience, anxious children are likely to be quiet, subdued, and eager to please. Many anxious children are overly compliant and exquisitely sensitive to interpersonal rejection. They are often perfectionistic and overachieving. These kids tend to be very "nice" and eager to please, and they are generally well liked by peers and adults. They may suffer quietly and may not come to anyone's attention for extended periods, despite distressing and impairing levels of anxiety.

Anxiety disorders tend to hang together. About 50% of children who meet criteria for one anxiety disorder meet criteria for two or more anxiety disorders. So, if one anxiety disorder is suspected, it's important to look for others. Anxious kids are at high risk for depression, too. About ⅓ of children with an anxiety disorder also have depression, so it's important to screen for it.

Because anxiety is a subjective internal state, it's important to interview the child directly. He or she may minimize symptoms in an effort to "look good" to the evaluator. Collateral information from parents and teachers is useful, as are classroom or playground observations. Anxious children tend to have higher than normal levels of somatic or physical complaints, such as headaches, stomachaches, and fatigue. This is particularly the case with children experiencing separation anxiety or performance anxiety, who are desperate to get home and access their primary attachment figures or avoid performance situations. There are several standardized self-rating scales available commercially, including the Revised Children's Manifest Anxiety Scale (Reynolds & Richmond, 1978) and the Multidimensional Anxiety Scale for Children (March, Parker, Sullivan, Stallings, & Conners, 1997). These are easy to use, self-scoring, and require no training to administer. They are excellent screening tools and can often give a good estimate of the level of anxiety, particularly in a child who is attempting to conceal symptoms. They can assist counselors in making decisions with regard to the need to refer to a higher level of care, and can enable counselors to follow children over time in order to assess progress in treatment.

INTERVENTIONS

Relaxation Training

Nearly all children—actually, probably all people—can benefit from relaxation training, so it's a good idea to provide it routinely with entire classes. What good is relaxation training? People who consistently practice relaxation on a daily basis, even just for a few minutes, reset their baseline level of anxiety. They become more relaxed overall throughout the day, every day, not just immediately after they perform the relaxation exercises. Also, these exercises are easy to learn and can be done independently, as they require no equipment and cost nothing. A child can be quietly seated in the classroom and be performing relaxation exercises and no one will know. After children become adept at achieving a state of deep relaxation, they can employ the exercises before they face a particularly stressful or scary situation, such as taking a big exam or presenting in front of a large group.

It is also important to point out to kids that when their anxiety becomes overwhelming, their ability to think, reason, or problem solve is compromised. It's as if their brain simply shuts off and is no longer of use to them. You can certainly recall an instance when you became so anxious your mind went blank and you got confused, disoriented, or forgetful. This impaired thinking is actually related to physiological changes that occur in the face of acute anxiety, which often triggers rapid, shallow breathing or hyperventilation. Rapid, shallow "chest" breathing, as it is sometimes called, is inefficient and alters blood chemistry such that it becomes more acidic which in turn triggers constriction of brain blood vessels. Hence, cognition is compromised.

Children (and adults) need to learn ways to lower their arousal to prevent brain "meltdowns" so that they might function better and cope with whatever situation they face.

An important point to make, especially with chronically stressed out or anxious kids, is that it may at first be very difficult for them to relax. Relaxation takes practice—lots and lots of practice for some. If children are used to carrying around a great deal of tension in their bodies and minds, it is difficult for them to break the habit. Warn them not to expect immediate results and encourage them to hang in there and just keep practicing daily. They should try to work these exercises into their daily routine, performing them for 15 minutes or so, every day and night. Kids can keep a relaxation log, as shown on page 144 in Appendix B. Some counselors make a relaxation tape for kids (duration 8 minutes, covering the three basic exercises detailed later in this section), which seems to work well. Finally, let them know that different techniques work well for different people. What usually works best, though, is to combine a few techniques, such as deep breathing, progressive muscle relaxation, and imagery.

There are lots of children with lots of worries and anxiety. Some studies estimate that perhaps as many as 15% of children suffer from an anxiety disorder, and anxiety disorders are becoming among the most prevalent of all disorders in children.

When you begin working with children with anxiety, you want to point out that some level of anxiety is normal and without it we'd be dead. So, too, some amount of anxiety spurs us to get things done and without it we'd lack motivation. However, anxiety can rise to the point that it causes suffering and impaired functioning.

Relaxation training is a good place to start when intervening with anxious youth. The three techniques to which children seem to respond the best are deep breathing, progressive muscle relaxation, and imagery. These scripts can be found on pages 145–146 in Appendix B.

Deep Breathing

You can explain that by simply changing the way we breathe, we can relieve our anxiety, stress, or anger. We actually change our body's chemistry when we adjust our breathing. Breathing slowly and deeply is the most efficient way to oxygenate our bodies and induces a relaxed state.

The first thing is to have kids sit or lie down on the floor an adequate distance away from each other. It's best if you can dim the lights some, make sure everyone is comfortable, and do your best to eliminate any interruptions or distractions. It's great if you can present this as a contest where we're going to try to be the most relaxed person in the room. It helps to offer a reward for the winner.

The script might go as follows:

Okay, are you all comfortable and have enough space from your neighbor? Now I want you to put your hand on your bellies and close your eyes. We're going to clear our minds and just concentrate on our breathing. We're going to learn how to take abdominal breaths, which is how newborn infants breathe. I want you to breathe in through your noses and take deep breaths, down into your abdomens. As you breathe in, you should feel your hand rising and falling. I'd like you to hold each breath for four seconds and then breathe out slowly, making a "whooshing" sound. Turn your mind to your breathing and tune in to your body. Clear your mind of any thoughts or worries. Now let's begin:

Take a deep breath in through your nose, slowly, deeply, and hold it, 1, 2, 3, 4. Now exhale slowly: whoooooosh (do it with them). That's one. Now again, deep breath in, hold it, 1, 2, 3, 4, exhale slowly, whoooooosh. That's two. (Repeat this with them for 10 cycles.)

Progressive Muscle Relaxation

You can share with children that it's been shown that sequentially tensing and then releasing muscles can help you achieve a state of deep relaxation. Again, ensure that kids are positioned comfortably with adequate space, free from interruptions or distractions, ideally in a quiet, softly lit environment. Again, it helps to model the exercises in front of them.

The script might go as follows:

Now I want you to squeeze your fists as tight as you can. Squeeze tight, hold it, 1, 2, tight, tighter, 3, 4, 5, 6, 7. Now release. Now tighten your biceps as much as you can by making a muscle with your arms. Hold it, 1, 2, tight, tight, tight, 3, 4, 5, 6, 7. Now release. Now tense your triceps by straightening your arms and locking your elbows. Hold it, tighter, 1, 2, 3, tighter still, hold it, 4, 5, 6, 7. Now release. Now tighten your neck muscles by arching your head down, trying to touch your chest with your nose. Hold it, 1, 2, 3, tighter, 4, 5, 6, 7. Now release. (You can have them arch their heads in each direction, front, back, left, and right because the neck particularly often carries a great deal of muscle tension). Now tense your shoulders by arching them back as if you were trying to touch them together. Arch them back, hard, hold it, tighter, 1, 2, 3, 4, 5, 6, 7. Now release. (You can repeat the tense-release of the shoulder blades because this is also often a problem area.) Now raise your shoulders up, as if you were going to touch your ears. Hold it, higher, 1, 2, 3, 4, 5, 6, 7. Now tighten your chest by taking in a deep breath and holding it, 1, 2, 3, 4, 5, 6, 7. Now release. Now tighten your belly muscles by sucking your tummy in. Suck in your tummies—that's it, hold, 1, 2, 3, 4, 5, 6, 7. Now release. Now tighten your bum. Squeeze those cheeks—hold it, squeeze, 1, 2, 3, 4, 5, 6, 7. Now release. Now tighten your thighs by straightening your legs out. Hold the tension in your legs, 1, 2, 3, 4, 5, 6, 7. Now release. Now curl your toes up, curl them as hard as you can—hold it, 1, 2, 3, 4, 5, 6, 7. Now release. Last one: Curl your toes down, into the floor—hold it, 1, 2, 3, 4, 5, 6, 7. Release.

Imagery

Imagery is a relaxation technique that children really like and respond to well. It's fun and allows them to use their imaginations. It works, because it is a form of distraction and interrupts a cycle of obsessive worrying. Further, imagery works because of emotional memories, especially if you can recruit them to help write the narrative for a peaceful scene. You can ask them to recall a fond or favorite memory of a place or event when they felt great. We can all recall shining or peaceful moments in our lives where we felt content, serene, or joyful. When you think back about the day your child was born, or the day you got that big promotion, you recall and actually reexperience the feelings you had at the time. For a child, an example might include a memory of lying around in the straw in the barn at Grandma's with some newborn kittens, building a sand castle on the beach, or going fishing with Dad. The counselor can play secretary and write down as vivid a description as possible of a favorite memory offered by a child to use for practicing imagery.

Ask children to get relaxed—maybe start with a few slow, deep breaths. Have them close their eyes and prepare to use their best imaginations. The script might go like this:

I want you to close your eyes and get ready to use your very best imagination. I really want you to go with me to the place I'm going to describe. Use all your senses and try hard to imagine the sights, sounds, smells, textures, and feelings that go along with the story.

You are visiting your Grandma at her farm. You just finished eating a hearty, warm lunch of grilled cheese sandwiches and tomato soup. You know how Grandma always spoils you! Your belly is just-right full and you feel completely satisfied. You're lying in a bed of straw in the barn. Smell that crisp country air with the smell of fresh straw and horses. You can hear the chickens clucking around outside. You nuzzle into the bed of straw and the barn kittens come out to play. They climb all over you and kiss your face with their sandpaper tongues. They purr and meow and wrestle with each other. This is a moment of pure bliss. You are at peace and wish this moment would never end.

You and your dad are sitting in the boat, leaning back, holding your fishing poles. You are in your favorite spot on the lake where the big fish bite. The sun is warm on your head and back but not too warm. The smell of lake water and the trees along the shore mix with the musty, fishy odor of your dad's fishing hat, which he is letting you wear. You can hear the sparrows chirping nearby and occasionally a fish jumps up to say hello. Your dad is so proud of you—you caught your first fish! A big catfish! Dad says you can take it home and Mom will serve it for dinner. The boat sways a little as the wind picks up. You watch the ripples in the lake as they build and fade. It's hypnotic. You feel so proud and warm and lucky. Now this is the life!

Somatic Desensitization

Anxious children, and anxious adults for that matter, tend to have what has been termed "anxiety sensitivity." This term has been coined to refer to the exquisite sensitivity anxious patients have to bodily cues.

Anxious kids note even mild somatic or bodily sensations, including the slightest vicissitude in heart rate, breathing, alertness, or gastrointestinal functioning. They tend to be hypervigilant with respect to their bodies and might make catastrophic attributions to irregular body sensations, such as chest tightness or difficulty catching a breath. In extreme cases, such as amidst a severe panic attack, an anxious child who experiences shortness of breath or chest pain might catastrophize that he or she is dying.

The DSM-IV diagnostic criteria for generalized anxiety disorder and panic disorder include physiological symptoms of anxiety such as restlessness, muscle tension, pounding or racing heart, sweating, trembling or shaking, and shortness of breath.

Before introducing relaxation exercises or techniques for cognitive restructuring, Flannery-Schroeder and Kendall (1996) suggest that it is helpful to teach kids to start paying attention to the bodily signals. You can model for children the physical experience of anxiety. For instance, you can ask them to imagine with you that you are facing a big test that you are nervous about. Perhaps you don't feel well prepared or lack confidence in the subject being tested. You start to have butterflies in your stomach and your thoughts are racing: "Oh no, what if I fail?!" Your hands are trembling and your body feels warm. You feel lightheaded and confused.

The idea is to help kids begin to note that they are experiencing increased anxiety and becoming at risk for a "meltdown." All people experience anxiety differently, but children struggling with anxiety should become adept at identifying their own body signals that they are entering a state of increased anxiety. After they are comfortable with catching themselves beginning to experience elevated physiological arousal, you can teach them tricks for lowering their arousal and aborting a full-blown anxiety attack early. Techniques include relaxation training, cognitive restructuring, and problem solving.

Cognitive Restructuring

This technique is geared primarily toward children 10 and over, but it has been used successfully in children as young as 8 or 9, who were high functioning and motivated for treatment.

Many kids who worry tend to have flawed thinking. They tend to overestimate the odds of bad things happening, catastrophize (or assume the worst), and underestimate their ability to cope with a bad outcome. They can get really locked into their negative thought patterns, and you can sometimes help them unlock by having them examine the evidence for their thoughts. The idea is to help children recognize that their feelings and behaviors grow out of their thinking. The goal is to help them recognize any distortions in their thinking and acknowledge and embrace the fact that they have the power to alter their thinking. This revelation alone can be enormously therapeutic and freeing to the anxious child.

Cognitive restructuring, along with relaxation training, constitutes much of what goes on in *cognitive behavioral therapy* (CBT). CBT is considered a first-line intervention for treating anxiety disorders in children and its efficacy and durability in this population has been documented in more than 16 controlled trials.

CBT has been studied empirically in both a group and individual format. It turns out that group CBT for pediatric anxiety is every bit as effective as individual CBT but, of course, group is a much more efficient mechanism for delivering intervention. Manuals for performing individual or group CBT for children with anxiety or depression are available commercially, including an empirically validated and widely used series by Kendall (2000).

A good place to start in helping anxious children unlock their negative and distorted thought patterns is familiarizing them with the common types of cognitive distortions that fuel anxiety. Similar lists of types of cognitive distortions are widely mentioned in self-help books for adults with anxiety or depression, such as those that appear in *The Feeling Good Handbook* by Burns (1999). The list that follows has been created and utilized successfully in the pediatric population. It can also be found on page 147 in Appendix B.

Types of Cognitive Distortions
Commonly Experienced by Anxious Children

Mindreading
Assuming you know what someone is thinking without checking.

Name-Calling
Using derogatory or pejorative labels to describe self or others (e.g., "He's a jerk or a liar or a loser" or "I'm so stupid or lazy or foolish").

Assuming the Worst

Convincing yourself that only the worst possible outcome will happen, when, in reality, the worst outcome is usually very unlikely (e.g., assuming that your friend didn't return your call because she no longer wants to be your friend, when it turns out she's sick in bed).

Overestimating the Chances of Something Bad

Assuming that a bad outcome is more likely than it really is (e.g., assuming you are going to fail a test because you studied only three nights, instead of four, even though you always do well in school).

Not Giving Yourself Enough Credit

Assuming you can't handle things when you really can (e.g., assuming you'd be devastated and unable to cope if you failed a class).

Seeing Things in Black and White

Viewing things as either all bad or all good, when most things and people are usually a mix of bad and good (e.g., assuming someone is a "total jerk" because he failed to say hello one morning).

Ignoring the Positive

Focusing entirely on the negative aspect of a situation and ignoring all the positive aspects (e.g., ruminating about getting 2 questions wrong, instead of 98 right).

The idea is to introduce children to the above types of distortions and reinforce the concepts by providing lots of examples and repeated exposures to the list. It may take some kids a great deal of repetition before they fully understand the nature of these distortions and are able to commit the list to memory. A useful next step is to encourage them to try to catch themselves using these distortions. Ask them to jot down examples of themselves or others employing a particular cognitive distortion and help them challenge their negative thoughts during sessions with you. You can model using distorted thinking and catching yourself so as to normalize the process and ensure that it is not shameful for them. Anxious children are usually exquisitely sensitive to criticism and rejection, which should be borne in mind at all times. They do not usually receive and tolerate negative or corrective feedback well.

You can gently point out examples of their distorted thinking as they share experiences to which they perhaps reacted in what appeared to be an unduly negative or unrealistic way. An example might be assuming that a peer who had bumped into an anxious child or passed by with a sour facial expression had hostile intentions. This is a classic example of *mindreading*. You can help these children recognize that a more likely explanation was that the peer had *accidentally* bumped into them or had a sour expression because of another event (recent scolding by a teacher) that had nothing to do with them.

Socratic Questions

Another simple technique for challenging distorted thinking is a series of Socratic questions. Most cognitive behavioral programs, including that by Bourne (1995), utilize such a list to assist anxious patients in challenging their negative thoughts. Familiarization and use of these questions help anxious children objectively examine situations and usually lead to a reappraisal of their assessments or perceptions and a diminution of their worries. A sample list of Socratic questions (also found on page 148 in Appendix B) includes the following:

Socratic Questions for Challenging Distorted Thinking
- *Has my fear come true before?*
- *What is the chance of my thought coming true?*
- *Are there any other ways this situation could turn out?*
- *What's the worst that could happen?*
- *How have I done in the past in similar situations?*
- *Can I think of any ways to cope with this situation?*
- *Am I underestimating my ability to deal with this situation?*

The Worry Game

You can create a game, tailored to an individual child, by making cards of their most common worries and other cards with Socratic questions. You then create a worry pile and a question pile with the cards. You can offer points, candy, or tokens for each answer. You can have the child take turns with you (or this can be done in a group), drawing a worry card and a question card, and answering the question in reference to the worry. A sample game appears here in Figure 4.1 and on page 149 in Appendix B.

Sample Worry Game

Directions: Cut out cards and divide into two piles: Socratic questions and worries. Take turns picking up a worry and a question and respond to the question for that particular worry. Give tokens or points for effort.

Positive Self-Talk

Children with excessive anxiety tend to engage in escalating, negative, sometimes catastrophic self-dialogue. For instance, they might say things to themselves such as, "Oh no, I'm going to fail this test, I'm going to get all the questions wrong, I'll fail second grade, oh no, oh no…." They should be encouraged to engage in more balanced positive self-talk, such as, "I may be nervous, but I can handle this test and I'll

What evidence is there for or against the worry?	Are there any other ways this situation could turn out?	What is the very worst that could happen? What is so bad about that? What would I do?
Has this worry come true or occurred before?	How have I done in the past in similar situations?	I'll get stuck in a stairwell
What is the chance my worry will come true?	I'll get a bad grade	I'll get stuck in an elevator
I might get hurt	I'll get in trouble	I'll get lost
My mom might get hurt	I might get beat up	I'll be embarrassed

FIGURE 4.1   SAMPLE WORRY GAME

probably at least pass like I have in the past." Another example might be a child thinking, "Oh no—I can't handle this; I've got to get out of here now!" That child could be coached to think differently, saying something like, "I may be uncomfortable, but I'm not in danger and I can handle this. I'll use my relaxation techniques to lower my anxiety and stay in control." Sometimes it is helpful to provide a list of so-called coping statements, such as the ones that follow (this list can also be found on page 148 in Appendix B):

Coping Statements
- *"Although I am uncomfortable, I can handle it."*
- *"Just breathe…"*
- *"This will pass…"*
- *"I have many ways to cope."*
- *"I can get help if I need it."*
- *"I am ready for a difficult situation."*
- *"I know what to do."*
- *"I have options."*

Thought Records

Thought records is a basic technique of cognitive behavior therapists, used to help anxious or depressed patients catch themselves using cognitive distortions and then restructure their thoughts and self-talk so their thinking becomes more realistic and balanced—that is, less anxiety provoking. Thought records appear in every cognitive therapy manual. A thought record used successfully with pediatric patients is shown in Figure 4.2, as well as on page 150 in Appendix B.

Exposure Therapy

Exposure therapy is the third component to CBT. Now armed with the tools of relaxation techniques and cognitive restructuring, the child can begin the process of desensitization through repeated exposures. With repeated exposures to a perceived threat or an anxiety-provoking situation, the child experientially learns that catastrophic predictions are not realized. The anxiety reaction to a particular environmental stimulus was learned, and was probably mostly born out of catastrophic or negative interpretations or thinking. So, too, anxiety runs a

---

Name:_____

Situation

Thoughts

Feelings

My Plan
(use relaxation,
challenge my thoughts,
get a buddy, face the
feared situation)

FIGURE 4.2   THOUGHT RECORD

---

course: It peaks, then extinguishes, over the course of a few minutes. If an anxiety-disordered youth can repeatedly face a threatening situation and ride out the anxiety, eventually the anxiety reaction will fade away. Better yet, a child who can learn to relax in the face of a previously anxiety-provoking stimulus will become re-conditioned or desensitized and will conquer the fear.

Exposure therapy is generally approached via what are termed *desensitization hierarchies,* which are typically mastered first in imagery and later in reality. To start, the counselor can sit down with the anxious child and select a particular feared situation. It's helpful to first pick the most anxiety-provoking image and make it the last step. Then have the child imagine a much less threatening, easily tolerated image and list that as Step 1. Then 6–8 steps can be added to the desensitization hierarchy between the two extremes identified. Coach the child to achieve deep relaxation, then have the child imagine the least threatening stimulus and stay with it as long as can be tolerated (stopping short of experiencing a moderate-severe level of anxiety). Then encourage the child to return to relaxation or envision a peaceful scene. The child can work through the imaginal hierarchy, alternating relaxation and peaceful scenes, over a course of a few weeks, if needed. After mastering the imaginal hierarchy, the child can tackle the real-life hierarchy, using the same basic exercises.

A sample desensitization hierarchy might look like Figure 4.3. A blank form for creating desensitization hierarchies can be found on page 151 in Appendix B.

The idea would be for the child to master the hierarchy in his or her imagination and then in real life. If the child is grappling with multiple feared situations, starting with an easy, confidence-building hierarchy before the child faces more challenging fears works well. It's helpful to build a reward system, so the child is motivated both intrinsically (out of the desire to get rid of anxiety and accomplish new things) and

---

Step 1: Imagine standing alone in the front of the classroom.

Step 2: Imagine standing alone in the front of the classroom and reading a passage from a book.

Step 3: Imagine reading a passage in front of a trusted friend or family member.

Step 4: Imagine standing up and introducing yourself to a small group of known peers.

Step 5: Imagine standing up and introducing yourself to a larger group, including strangers.

Step 6: Imagine sharing a favorite poem or story with a small group.

Step 7: Imagine sharing a personal story with a larger group, including strangers.

Step 8: Imagine giving a speech or formal presentation to a large crowd of strangers.

FIGURE 4.3   HIERARCHY FOR FEAR OF PUBLIC SPEAKING

extrinsically (having something fun to look forward to and show for all the effort).

Consider the following example:

Kaylen was the type of fourth-grade student who is often overlooked in the classroom. Eager to please and socially timid, her behavior at school did not grab the attention of her teachers. It was at the request of her mother that Kaylen presented to the school counselor. Kaylen's mother had intercepted a letter to a teen magazine articulating her extraordinary fear and anguish of punishment.

Kaylen's mother contacted the school requesting an evaluation by the school psychologist. In a very brief interview, it was clear that Kaylen was suffering from unusual cognitive distortions. Kaylen had recently seen a TV documentary that uncovered "unfair and abusive" punishments that children suffered at the hands of otherwise "trustworthy" child-care and educational providers. Kaylen had begun to obsess about the victims and imagine her own vulnerability to suffer similar offenses.

Kaylen had been traumatized by the documentary, and she admitted that although she had never herself suffered unjustly, she obsessively worried that something terrible was going to happen to her at the hands of her teachers or caregivers.

Fortunately, Kaylen's suffering was short-lived. She responded well to psychoeducation regarding cognitive distortions and anxiety. The school psychologist helped her realize that the odds that she would experience something that she had witnessed on TV were extremely low. She soon recognized the pattern of her distorted thoughts and learned to abort these thoughts midstream and redirect her thinking.

RECOMMENDATIONS FOR THE CLASSROOM

Counselors can encourage teachers to regularly cue children with excessive anxiety, using a predetermined signal, to take a deep breath or relax and stretch their muscles. This may help children release some tension so that they can refocus on their academic material. Anxious children are often prone to temper outbursts: Anxiety is closely linked to aggression and both reactions are adrenaline fueled. Kids with temper outbursts, too, can be helped by cues from teachers to take "cool downs" and practice relaxation when stressed or frustrated.

Children with anxiety disorders tend to have low self-esteem and be highly sensitive to criticism and prone to self-deprecation. Teachers can help them by finding opportunities to offer specific praise and encouragement. Also, they can look for chances to involve these children in a special way in classroom activities, such as assigning them special jobs, errands, or leadership roles. However, teachers should bear in mind that anxious children don't feel comfortable when excessive public attention is focused on them, so efforts should be made to transmit information, especially if sensitive or embarrassing, privately. Children with anxiety respond best when spoken to in a soft voice in a nonthreatening manner.

The Selectively Mute Child: What to Do With Kids Who Won't Talk at School

— by Mary Cook, MD

EPIDEMIOLOGY AND MAJOR CHARACTERISTICS

A child who refuses to talk at all while at school is actually relatively rare, compared to other types of behavioral and emotional problems. Often the school staff and parents are at a loss as to how to intervene when a child refuses to talk. The official psychiatric term for children refusing to speak in select environments (not due to inability to speak) is selective mutism.

Selective mutism has been conceptualized as a form of social phobia. The hallmark of the disorder is a refusal to speak in specific settings, such as the classroom, while talking in other settings, such as the home. In one study, 90% of children with selective mutism also meet criteria for social phobia. Prevalence rates of 0.3 to 0.8 per 1,000 have been reported, making this a relatively rare disorder. Selective mutism appears to afflict girls at a rate equal to boys, although one study found a girl: boy ratio of 2:1. The characteristic family dynamics associated with selective mutism include an overly enmeshed relationship between mother and child with the mother perhaps being overprotective and overindulgent toward the child. The marital relationship is often conflictual, with the father often ineffectual and distant.

A child refusing to speak at school needs aggressive intervention as early as possible. Early intervention leads to a good prognosis and more rapid recovery. Children need to speak at school to keep up with academic achievement and to develop socially. It is essential that they speak at school. The longer a child is selectively mute, the more refractory they become to intervention. As the condition persists for longer periods, the behavioral pattern becomes more deeply ingrained; interventions are less likely to work and take longer to have an effect.

Children who are selectively mute often come from families who are very close. You are likely to find a pattern of parents behaving in an extremely protective manner and perhaps inadvertently or overtly communicating to the child that the world is an unsafe place. You often hear from parents that the selectively mute child is usually very talkative in select settings, such as at home or in the homes of very familiar relatives or friends.

INTERVENTIONS

Contingency Management, Stimulus Fading, and Response Initiative Procedures

Some basic strategies for intervening with selective mutism include contingency management, stimulus fading with positive reinforcement, and response initiative procedures. Contingency management refers to the use of positive reinforcement for verbal behaviors and nonreinforcement or extinction of nonverbal requests (pointing or mouthing). This works best if there is already at least some speech present across settings. Stimulus fading refers to offering rewards to the child for first speaking to the teacher in the home, then en route to school, then on the playground, and finally in the classroom. Other adults and children are slowly added to the mix, and time-outs are applied for mutism. Response initiative procedures involve first "shaping," which refers to first asking the child to mouth, blow, or whisper words. Positive reinforcement or rewards are offered for compliance, and the sophistication of the level of speech behavior required for rewards is gradually increased. Mutism results in a response cost or revoking of rewards, and children are timed out until they emit at least one word at school.

It's important to inform the child's classmates about his or her condition in a positive, supportive way. An intervention that is extremely helpful to start things off is to have parents bring in a video of a child who is selectively mute at school chatting away at home. This intervention should be discussed in advance with the child and the counselor should ensure she or he is agreeable to it. When addressing the class (in the child's presence), the parents and teacher should be careful to present the video and their concerns regarding the child's failure to speak in a gentle, nonshaming way. The message conveyed to the class should essentially be, "Hey, Susie *can* speak, but she simply finds it extremely difficult in the school setting. She has a fear of speaking, just like some people have a fear of spiders or heights." It turns out peers or classmates of selectively mute children often assume that the child is *not capable* of speaking—that there is something wrong with the child.

Two programs that worked well are described as follows in the form of case vignettes:

Jeff was a 6-year-old boy, the youngest of two children from an intact family. Jeff's parents were extremely devoted and protective. They spent a great deal of time together as a family and encouraged Jeff and his older sister to play together, almost exclusively. When the family did venture out, they usually spent time only with familiar friends and relatives, doing familiar activities. The parents used extreme caution in arranging any kind of play dates for their children and always insisted that the two siblings accompany one another to a friend's house. Jeff spoke freely at home and in the homes of familiar people.

During Jeff's first year of school, he did not utter a word unless certain no one but a family member was present. His father described him chattering away en route to school but abruptly falling silent upon stepping onto school grounds.

The interventions applied at the start of his second year of school, when he remained mute, involved a great deal of collaboration between Jeff's teacher, parents, classmates, and the consulting pediatric mental health providers.

The first step was for the parents, in Jeff's presence, to share with the class a video of him chattering away at home. Jeff's classmates were shocked to learn that he was perfectly capable of talking and, in fact, could be quite talkative. The class had assumed that Jeff couldn't talk. It was explained to the class that Jeff felt uncomfortable talking at school and would need their help to begin doing so.

A point chart for Jeff was developed and posted openly in the classroom. A list of behavioral targets, involving progressive levels of speech, was generated. Only one target at a time, introduced at a pace of about one per week, was shared with Jeff and the class.

The program was very simple and involved awarding one point each time the week's target was met.

It was clear that the thought of speaking in the school setting was very anxiety provoking for Jeff and therefore the rewards selected needed to have a high valence. His father suggested an Xbox, a $150 piece of video game equipment, over which the child had been drooling for months. It was determined that the Xbox would be worth 100 points. The points were carefully tracked on a board posted conspicuously at school and on a chart at home. A system of cards with point totals was developed to ensure communication between teacher and parents.

Peer pressure was also a tactic. The goal of helping Jeff become comfortable speaking was presented as a project that would involve the entire class, which was promised a pizza party as soon as 100 points were achieved.

A storyboard was developed by the class with photos depicting Jeff and his classmates achieving each new milestone of verbal communication. Lots of praise and positive attention were showered on Jeff and the class by peers, teachers, and parents as greater levels of speech were achieved.

A list of progressive behavioral targets was developed as follows, with consideration of the fact that Jeff had not been known to utter a word to anyone (other than family when alone) at school in the past:

Week 1: Jeff is to mouth words. (This was continued for one week, with Jeff being awarded one point for each instance of mouthing a word. Classmates would often witness these instances and alert the teacher excitedly of Jeff's success, which they also perceived as their success and ticket to a pizza party.)

Week 2: Jeff is to whisper words in someone's ear. The same rules mentioned in Week 1 applied.

Week 3: Jeff is to whisper words out loud, such that someone standing an arm's length away can hear and discern what he is saying.

Week 4: Jeff is to say words sufficiently loud so that someone standing 5–10 feet away can hear.

Week 5: Jeff is to speak loudly enough to be heard from across the room.

Finally, Jeff was taught relaxation exercises, which he was cued to use any time he experienced elevated anxiety.

This program was extremely successful. Jeff had been well known for being mute, and he had been receiving some caretaking behavior from teachers and parents, which had inadvertently perpetuated his mutism. For instance, if he needed an eraser, he would point to one and the teacher would give it to him. During the administration of this program, the teachers and parents required Jeff to at least mouth words, and later speak them, to be able to get his needs met. He could not ask for a particular food at the lunch line or to go to the bathroom without employing verbal communication.

Because the class was on board from the beginning and Jeff's problems with speaking had been discussed openly, the class eagerly embraced their self-appointed mission to help Jeff get over his fear. Moreover, the teacher, other students, Jeff, and his parents were united in their goal, with a pizza party reward for all upon mission completion. The other interventions, such as the storyboard with pictures chronicling Jeff's progress and the prominently displayed sticker chart documenting his point accumulation, were very powerful constant reminders of the mission.

By the end of two months, Jeff was speaking freely and in fact, his teacher complained in jest, "Now I can't shut him up!" The teacher received a cash award and official letter of recognition for her efforts in helping this child achieve greater social and academic success.

Maria was a 5-year-old girl from a close intact family. She had a younger brother and large extended family with whom she had regular contact. She refused to speak outside of her home since toddlerhood. This obviously became of great concern when she started school.

Maria's program consisted initially of working individually with a counselor. A token jar and sticker board were created for her. She was asked to carry the token jar with her at all times and the sticker board was maintained in a conspicuous place at home. Initially, Maria was coaxed to at least whisper to her mother in the presence of the counselor. For each instance of whispering, she received a token. Later, the tokens were traded in for rewards. The program consisted of continuous reinforcement, with both immediate and longer-term rewards and praise, and a progressive hierarchy of efforts in speaking to familiar people and, later, less familiar people. Maria developed an awards menu with her parents as follows:

Small Reward (10 Tokens) = Chooses and watches a video rental

Medium Reward (20 Tokens) = Family goes to her favorite restaurant for dinner

Large Reward (30 Tokens) = Family goes to the zoo

The program went as follows:

Session 1: Maria was asked to whisper to her mother in the counselor's presence and received one token for each instance of compliance.

Session 2: Maria was asked to read a book aloud to her mother in the counselor's presence. Same reward system as above.

Session 3: Maria was asked to whisper to the counselor in her mother's presence.

Session 4: Maria was asked to read a book to the counselor in her mother's presence.

Session 5: Maria was asked to speak on the phone to her mother, who called from a different room, in the counselor's presence.

Session 6: Maria was asked to speak on the phone to an unfamiliar person with the counselor, but not her mother, present.

Session 7: Maria was asked to speak on the phone to her mother in her teacher's presence.

Session 8: Maria was asked to whisper to her teacher in the presence of a few peers.

Session 9: Maria was asked to speak to her teacher loud enough to hear at arm's length in the presence of a few peers.

This program too was successful and had the child speaking normally at school with familiar and unfamiliar people within two months. The key to success seemed to be the stepwise progression of demands and the combination of short- and long-term rewards.

Figure 5.1 shows a sample behavioral contract for selective mutism, which can also be found on pages 161–162 in Appendix D. Typically, the child, her parents, and the teacher would negotiate and sign such a contract. Counselors can suggest another meeting after two weeks to modify the program and review progress.

Target Behaviors:

1. "I will speak to my friends at recess."
2. "I will speak to my parents on the phone in the classroom."
3. "I will use words to communicate at the youth center." (Other targets could be used, such as, "I will mouth the words I'd like to say," "I will speak to my teacher in a whisper," and later, "I will speak to my teacher loud enough to be heard two feet away," and so on.) No more than three targets should be attempted at once.

Special Arrangements:

1. The mother or father will call each day at _____ on the classroom phone.
2. After first week, teacher assigns _____ a buddy for recess to count words.
3. Classmates and youth center workers are aware of the program.

Tracking:

1. _____ receives one point per word spoken at recess or on the phone with parents in the classroom or spoken at any time to any peer/teacher/daycare provider on school grounds or at the youth center.
2. An outgoing buddy will be appointed each day by the teacher to count words spoken at recess.
3. The teacher will write the number of words/points earned on the chalkboard at the end of recess each day and record it on a card to be sent home.
4. The youth center workers will write the number of words/points on a card each day.
5. _____'s parents will give one penny for each point earned.

Rewards/Consequences:

1. Parents will not continue phone calls to classroom if _____ fails to speak at all on phone in classroom when they call at designated time.
2. After 50 points are earned, the class has a party (movie, popcorn, the works!).
3. Rewards Menu (provided at home by parents):
   Small—20 Points/Pennies (e.g., small toy, pizza, ice cream):
   _____

   Medium—40 Points/Pennies (e.g., bowling, movies, dinner out):
   _____

   Large—60 Points/Pennies (e.g., zoo, theme park, Xbox):
   _____

FIGURE 5.1   BEHAVIORAL CONTRACT FOR A SELECTIVELY MUTE CHILD

The School-Refusing Child: What to Do When Kids Won't Go to School

—by Mary Cook, MD

EPIDEMIOLOGY AND MAJOR CHARACTERISTICS

Nearly 30% of school-aged children refuse school at one time or other. This behavior occurs equally in boys and girls. Peak age of occurrence is 10–13, but there are also peaks at ages 5–6 and 14–15 as children enter new schools. School refusal can manifest in a myriad of ways. School refusal is commonly associated with separation anxiety, generalized anxiety, social anxiety, and depression, and can show up as complaints or expression of fear and somatic complaints (headaches, stomachaches, and fatigue). Other possible expressions of school refusal might include tantrums, aggression, clinging, refusal to move, running away, and noncompliance.

There are significant consequences for school refusal, and the longer it goes untreated the more refractory it becomes. The short-term impact might include child and family stress, legal problems, deteriorating academic and social functioning, and potential child maltreatment and lack of supervision. Long-term consequences include lower academic achievement, decreased higher education opportunities, occupational and marital problems, substance abuse, and criminality.

In assessing a child with school refusal, it's important to identify the major trigger or etiology for the behavior. The most common reason for school refusal is separation anxiety, where a child becomes extremely anxious when forced to separate from a parent or other caregiver. Extreme cases of separation anxiety can approach the level of panic, and the child may go to great lengths to avoid a separation. A child may also be avoiding school to avoid a bully or harsh teacher or may be concerned about humiliation related to learning or social impairments. So, too, the child may desire increased closeness and special attention from significant others. Sometimes kids have discovered that if they stay home, especially when feigning illness, they can sleep in, watch television, or play video games. Or they may get lots of TLC from their mom or dad. Often, older kids ditch school to spend time with friends, pursuing more pleasurable activities. Identifying the root cause or motivation for the school refusal is key to developing an effective intervention plan.

The trick is to nip this problem in the bud. Advise parents that no matter how loudly their child protests, they must insist that the child attend school. After all, it is the law. The exception, of course, would be if there are objective signs of genuine illness, such as excessive vomiting, cough, or fever, or if a doctor has said the child needs to stay home.

The presentation is often of a child complaining of lots of vague, nonspecific somatic or bodily complaints such as headaches or stomachaches or fatigue. Often, especially if there is extreme anxiety about attending school, the child might tantrum loudly en route to school, sometimes even becoming physically combative. It is usually difficult for parents, especially mothers, to tolerate these tantrums, and they feel uncomfortable pressing the child to attend school. If a child has separation anxiety, usually so does the parent. There is usually a dynamic between parent and child whereby neither the child nor the parent tolerate separation from one another. Again, collaboration between parents, school staff, and consulting pediatric mental health providers is key to success.

INTERVENTIONS

Kearny and Albano (2000) have developed a program for parents and therapists for addressing school refusal, titled *When Children Refuse School*. Because this program is comprehensive and commercially available, the interventions discussed here will be based on my clinical experiences and are limited to cases of school refusal secondary to separation anxiety.

The following example is a commonly occurring observed phenomenon that occurs in nearly all schools at the start of kindergarten each year:

Arriving each morning a few minutes after the morning bell had rung, Shelly was already at an immediate disadvantage. She was a child who tended to have difficulty with transitions, and running late each morning left her ill at ease. To make matters worse, her father would inevitably linger 15–30 minutes before forcing a separation. The longer he stayed and the more reservation he expressed regarding leaving, the more difficult it became for Shelly to separate. When at last he would insist that he had to go or be in trouble at work, Shelly would collapse into tears, often clinging to his pant leg. Although her father was reassured by the school staff that Shelly would be fine once he left, he clearly had doubts that were obvious even to Shelly. He struggled with his own ambivalence regarding leaving his daughter at school, and his ambivalence and anxiety clearly fueled that of his daughter, compounding the problem.

When Shelly's behavior continued into her third week of school, a plan was quickly devised—for her father. Gently and tactfully, he was counseled regarding the need to change his morning behavior with Shelly. He was reassured that his behavior was not uncommon, but was nonetheless advised that it was not helpful and was likely sabotaging efforts at helping Shelly adjust to school and tolerate separation from him. He was asked to have Shelly arrive ten minutes before the first morning bell. During this time, he was invited to enter the classroom, explore the day's activities, and so on. However, he was persuaded to take the sound of the first morning bell as his cue to leave the classroom. This plan was discussed with Shelly and a ritual hug and handshake was developed between them. Although Shelly predictably cried on the first several days as he kept his promise to exit, she soon adjusted. Delighted finally to be able to say good-bye without an emotional scene, Shelly's father began to experience security in the system, and as he became more confident, Shelly became more confident as well. Eventually, he was able to drop her at the front curb where she eagerly joined her classmates.

The next two case vignettes describe David's garden-variety case of school refusal followed by Jeremy's more unusual case, which developed after a relatively traumatic event.

David, a 6-year-old Caucasian boy, was the youngest of four siblings and had always been babied by his family. He was very large for his age and stood out from his peers because of his size. He was also a slow learner and had been diagnosed with a reading disorder.

David began missing more and more school and his mother began missing more and more work as a result of his progressive tantrumming every morning when his mother attempted to drop him off at school.

Observations of the morning drop-offs revealed that David whined, cried, and ran after his mother. She became progressively more anxious, distraught, and frustrated, and had concerns about losing her job. She responded to his protests with a great deal of empathy, nurturance, and pleading. When David was left at school, he usually made his way to the school nurses, complaining of stomachaches or fatigue. His mother would be called and invited to pick him up, which she did. However, it was noted that on occasions when David remained in school, he did fine. He did not seem anxious or distressed in any way and participated normally in classroom activities.

It became clear that his mother's behavior was reinforcing and maybe even causing David's school refusal. Alternative arrangements were made, whereby David was dropped off by his father, sister, or daycare provider. Further, the teachers and nurse agreed not to send David home, even if he whined, cried, or feigned sickness. Still the tantrumming and running away persisted.

The strategy next employed is a form of forced school attendance. It may seem a little unorthodox to some readers, but it worked like a charm in this case. When David attempted to run from school, he was carried, like a sack of potatoes, into his class. When he attempted to run out of the room, the door was held shut. The teacher and classmates were advised to ignore his tantrumming and carry on with their work as usual. David tantrummed for 20 minutes at the door the first day and 15 minutes or so the second, but by the end of the week, he dutifully entered the class without protest.

The above program was successful. It became clear that David could tolerate separation from his mother without undue distress. His tantrums were being rewarded with nurturing behavior and, in many instances, a trip home. When the rewards were removed and it was made clear to David that he would be required to stay at school regardless of the size of his tantrum, his school refusal resolved.

Jeremy was a 9-year-old Caucasian boy who came from a close-knit family and had been raised in a small, safe, sheltered community. His mother was a teacher, and his father was a minister. Jeremy was previously described as outgoing and confident. He operated very independently and warmed up to new people and situations easily.

His behavior and attitudes changed significantly in the context of moving to a larger community, having his father quit the ministry, and getting stuck in an elevator for several hours by himself. Immediately after the incident of being stuck in the elevator, Jeremy regressed significantly and exhibited significant separation anxiety for the first time. He could not tolerate separation from his mother and would whine and tantrum anytime a separation was threatened. His parents were alarmed by his behaviors and did not force any separations. In fact, his mother was a teacher at the same school he attended and she, although he was assigned to a different class, had allowed him to remain in her classroom.

When school administrators learned he was staying in his mother's classroom, they insisted that immediate action be taken and that separation be forced. However, an immediate and abrupt forced separation made the parents and child very uncomfortable. Instead, a graduated separation, with a system of rewards for tolerating separation, was planned.

The approach to intervening with any fear, phobia, or anxiety is graduated exposure to the stimulus that is anxiety provoking. At the same time, the child is taught relaxation techniques to use when exposed to the stimulus. In this case, it was sufficient to schedule a series of contacts between child and parent throughout the day. The teachers and parents were coached to behave in a matter-of-fact, reassuring way, even when the child deteriorated and tantrummed. The team was advised to adhere to the contract developed in consultation with the child, even if he begged for increased contact. Each week, the amount of contact was diminished. There was a system of tokens developed, by which Jeremy could earn rewards for compliance. The contract was as follows:

Week 1: Jeremy could sit in a chair, immediately outside the door of his mother's classroom, for 10 minutes out of every hour. He was not allowed to speak to his mother or disrupt her or the class in any way. For contingencies, in the event that Jeremy felt he could not tolerate waiting until the scheduled time, he was given three emergency cards. He could trade these cards for an opportunity to walk by his mother's class and peek in to assure himself she was there and in good health. However, if he didn't use his emergency cards, he could cash them in with his parents for money, 25 cents per card. If he stayed beyond his 10 allotted minutes, he had to pay 25 cents. (Jeremy never used up any of these cards.)

Week 2: Jeremy could sit in a chair, immediately outside his mother's classroom, for 10 minutes at three scheduled times throughout the day (morning, lunch, and midafternoon). The same rules as above applied.

Week 3: Jeremy could sit twice for a period of 10 minutes as already described.

Week 4: Jeremy's scheduled visits outside his mother's classroom were replaced with scheduled phone calls, carefully timed so they wouldn't disrupt her work.

Over the next two weeks, Jeremy was weaned from his phone calls. He was encouraged to practice relaxation when he became anxious about separation. He was left with contingency cards, which he never used.

Jeremy used the money he earned by saving his contingency cards to buy toys with his parents each week. A similar system of graduated separations, with scheduled phone calls and rewards for tolerating separation, was developed and implemented at home.

The program outlined above was successful, and within two months, Jeremy showed no evidence of separation anxiety or school refusal. This case of separation anxiety and refusal to attend school in an assigned classroom was unique because the mother was accessible at the school. In the event that the mother, who is almost always the object of separation anxiety, worked outside the school or in the home, a similar system of graduated separation could be developed. If available, the mother could be sitting in the school library where the child could walk by and spot her at scheduled times. Or the child could be issued a series of scheduled phone appointments, of brief duration (say two minutes or less), from which he would be gradually weaned. A reward system for compliance, especially when the rewards are of high value to the child, increases the chances for success.

The Disruptive or ADHD Child: What to Do When Kids Won't Sit Still and Be Quiet

—by Mary Cook, MD

*S*uccessful intervention for severely disruptive children is likely to require effort and collaboration between pediatric mental health specialists, parents, and school staff. Children with severe disruptive behavior disorders usually require follow-up with credentialed pediatric mental health specialists and may need special classrooms, schools, or even residential treatment centers. Still, school counselors often find themselves as the first line of defense with these children. Children who disrupt the classroom may have a variety of psychiatric disorders, including attention deficit hyperactivity disorder (ADHD), oppositional defiant disorder (ODD), and conduct disorder (CD).

ATTENTION DEFICIT HYPERACTIVITY DISORDER

The usual figure for prevalence for ADHD is 3% to 5% of school-aged children (Cantwell, 1996). It is fairly clear from genetic and brain imaging studies that ADHD is a brain disorder, not a disorder caused by parenting or other environmental factors. ADHD clearly runs in families, with heritability estimates ranging from .55 to .92. On average, 25% of immediate family members of children with ADHD are likely to have the disorder. Put another way, there is a 50% chance that one of the ADHD child's parents will also have the disorder. Psychosocial factors are not thought to play a primary etiological role.

Studies reveal that stimulant medications are a robust and safe treatment for ADHD with no significant long-term ill effects, including no significant impact on growth. Some studies have even revealed that stimulant medications used for ADHD may have a protective effect in terms of decreasing the risk of substance abuse in treated ADHD patients, when compared to their untreated counterparts. The core criteria for ADHD come in two categories: inattentive and impulsive-hyperactive criteria. They include disorganization, distractibility, forgetfulness, tendency to lose things, seeming not to listen, overactivity, fidgetiness, excessive talkativeness, failure to remain seated, blurting things out, and interrupting.

Children with ADHD are likely to have comorbid psychiatric disorders, including learning disabilities, ODD, CD, anxiety, depression, and substance abuse. Up to 65% of children with ADHD are likely to have ODD as well. It is important, after an ADHD diagnosis has been established, to rule out other diagnostic entities. At the school in particular, the child should be assessed for a learning impairment. Children with ADHD are also likely to be rejected socially: They tend to misinterpret social cues in an overly hostile way, interrupt, butt ahead, refuse to follow game rules, and make offensive remarks impulsively. Studies reveal that children with comorbid problems, particularly social impairment, anxiety, and oppositionality, are likely to benefit from the addition of intensive behavior modification.

The clinical lore used to be that ADHD children outgrew their disorder. Studies now reveal that this lore was false, that children do seem to outgrow the hyperactivity symptoms, which begin dissipating around age 11, as well as their impulsivity symptoms, which typically begin to fade around age 13. But a significant portion of children with ADHD—perhaps half—continue to manifest clinically significant levels of inattention into adolescence and young adulthood.

OPPOSITIONAL DEFIANT DISORDER

Like ADHD, ODD tends not to occur by itself. Up to 80% of children with ODD also have ADHD. ODD children are likely to also have problems with learning, anxiety, or depression, or may go on to develop conduct disorder. ODD is found in 5% to 15% of school-aged boys and 1% to 4% of school-aged girls, demonstrating a clear predilection for afflicting boys. The criteria for ODD include a negativistic, hostile attitude, tendency to lose temper, argumentativeness, defiance, deliberate annoying of others, and vindictiveness. ODD children are at higher risk to develop conduct disorder, a more serious disorder associated with criminality, substance abuse, and violation of the rights of others.

Two empirically validated intensive behavioral programs currently are available for the treatment of ODD. These include *parent management training* (Barkley, 1997) and *collaborative problem solving* (Greene, 2001). The program developed by Greene is particularly designed for implementation in the schools, although a manual for his program is not yet available.

CONDUCT DISORDER

Conduct disorder, like ODD, tends to affect more boys than girls, with prevalence rates of 5% to 16% in school-aged boys, versus 1% to 4%

in girls. The hallmarks of CD are bullying, physical fights, using a weapon, cruelty to animals and people, forced sexual activity, property destruction, lying, stealing, fire setting, truancy, and running away. CD, as well as ODD, is more prevalent in families of lower socioeconomic status. Several psychiatric disorders are associated with CD, including ADHD, substance abuse, depression, mania, schizophrenia, and ultimately, antisocial personality disorder, which is roughly equivalent to sociopathy. Depression in particular is highly associated with CD, with some studies quoting rates of up to 60% of youth with CD having comorbid depression. The prognosis for conduct disorder, especially with onset before age 10, is bleak. Children with conduct disorder, especially if they develop comorbid depression or substance abuse problems, are likely to be refractory to intervention and are at higher risk for legal, occupational, and marital problems. Early, aggressive, multimodal intervention affords the best prognosis for youth with CD.

ASSESSMENT

The worst source of information for children suspected of having impulse control or disruptive behavior problems is the children themselves. Children with disruptive behavior disorders tend to be emotionally immature and lack insight regarding their behaviors and feelings. They tend to externalize or have an external locus of control, and typically blame teachers, parents, peers, or the dog for their misbehavior or academic failure. They have difficulty taking personal responsibility for their behavior and recognizing any role they might have played in a conflict situation. They tend to misinterpret social cues in general, and in particular they are likely to interpret neutral stimuli in an overly negative, hostile, or threatening way. For instance, a child with ADHD or ODD is more likely to assume hostile intent when bumped in line by a peer than does a child without ADHD.

Of course, interviewing the child provides some useful information. In particular, it helps the evaluator understand the child's perspective, feelings, concerns, and psychological defenses. In terms of collecting data to support a disruptive behavior disorder, the best investment is in collateral sources, that is, obtaining feedback from teachers and parents or other caregivers. Direct classroom or playground observations can be helpful, too, but are not always feasible or practical.

Rating scales such as the Parent and Teacher Conners Scales (Conners, 1997) and the Child Behavior Checklist (Achenbach & Edelbrock, 1991) are very valuable in assessing for disruptive behaviors and associated symptoms. These are commercially available, easy to use, and require no special training. They can be obtained initially as part of a preliminary work-up and repeated over time to assess response to treatment—in particular medication treatment of ADHD.

As mentioned previously, children with ADHD are at risk for learning disorders. It is therefore important to screen those who are struggling academically for learning disabilities.

INTERVENTIONS

Disruptive children often have problems getting along with adults and peers. They typically have problem-solving deficits and trouble controlling their anger. They often misinterpret social cues and annoy and offend others. Therefore, disruptive children would benefit from the social skills training covered in Chapter 4, "The Socially Impaired Child." In particular, they struggle with expressing negative feelings in a safe and appropriate way and resolving social conflict. Assertiveness training is extremely helpful for these children (covered in Chapter 4). You can suggest to these disruptive children that they will be more successful at getting what they want and keeping friends if they learn to use their words and not their fists to vent anger. In addition, children with a pattern of explosive anger can be taught relaxation techniques to control their anger and can be cued to "take a cool down" when they are beginning to get agitated. The following interventions are also helpful.

Anger Management Training

Initially, when working with children who are thought to have anger management problems that show up in the form of tantrums, verbal or physical aggression, or property destruction, the key is to understand as much as possible about the child and his or her anger triggers. Anger and fear or anxiety are thought to be closely linked reactions and both produce an adrenaline response. Anger might be thought of as fear or anxiety turned out and anxiety might be thought of as anger turned in. Essentially, kids (and adults) express anger when they feel threatened. When they fear their needs won't get met, they get mad.

Kids who are at risk for having problems with inappropriate and explosive expression of anger include those with ADHD because they are impulsive and often don't think before they react. Also at risk are kids with learning problems and language delays. These children might not have the words to communicate their needs effectively or the know-how to get what they need in an adaptive way. Children with autism often exhibit explosive aggression, probably secondarily to their limited language abilities.

You can begin by talking to the parents, teacher, and the child to learn about that child's particular triggers. Performing classroom and playground observations can also be helpful.

When you begin with a child or group of children, begin by talking about anger in general. You want to be clear that experiencing anger, even on a daily basis, is perfectly normal. You want to be sure they don't become ashamed about their anger and that they understand that expression of anger is normal and healthy. You can tell them that to experience transient wishes to harm others, in the heat of anger, is perfectly normal and common. They can fantasize about anything they want, just so long as wishes to harm others remain a fantasy. Tell them about ambivalence in relationships, that is, that we all sometimes feel angry even at people we love. All relationships and all people are a mix of good and bad, and just because we sometimes get angry, even at people we love, doesn't mean we're bad or that we don't love someone.

Ask them if anger is ever a good thing. Ask for examples. They should arrive at the notion that anger is sometimes helpful and fuels change. If we're mad enough about an injustice, we work hard to try to make things right. You can bring up examples from history, such as the actions of Rosa Parks and Martin Luther King, Jr.

Have the child or group of children brainstorm a list of signals that cue them that they're angry.

The list might look like this:

My face turns red.

I feel sick to my stomach.

My fists ball up.

I get sweaty.

I clench my teeth.

I want to kill somebody.

My muscles tense up.

I start screaming.

The idea is to help kids recognize anger early and identify patterns in their development of anger. What kinds of things set them off? Again, here's an opportunity to point out how we all perceive the same situation differently and different things make different people angry. Many kids with explosive aggression and severe tantrums find it difficult to de-escalate their reactions after they've blown a fuse. The idea is to be proactive in identifying anger triggers and heading them off before they escalate. Also, if children become more tuned into their body signals, they can take care of themselves and deal with the anger and the precipitant for their anger before they blow.

Ask kids to give examples of explosive anger from their own experiences or imaginations. Write each example on the board and have them generate a list of potential long-term and short-term consequences, both positive and negative, for each instance of explosive aggression.

The next step is to teach them some immediate ways of getting control of their anger, before it builds to the point of no return. Relaxation training is invaluable for children with explosive anger. It is a must for all kids who undergo anger management training. Children respond wonderfully to the techniques detailed in Chapter 4, "The Anxious Child." They should be encouraged to practice relaxation daily, which will result in a lowering of their baseline level of tension, and to employ relaxation when they begin to feel angry or anxious. You can point out that these exercises require no equipment and are free. Children can be cued by parents and teachers initially (the idea is for them to eventually cue themselves) to take a "cooldown" (sounds better than "time-out," which has punitive implications).

Problem-Solving Skills Training

Problem-solving skills are especially important for children who have trouble with inappropriate expressions of anger. After children have taken a cooldown and feel in control enough to reason and talk, they can be encouraged to problem solve. When they are ready to problem solve around a social conflict, the counselor's role should be to guide and support, but *not direct*. The idea is to guide the child to become an independent thinker and problem-solver who makes good choices, whether you're in the room or not. The counselor can introduce the steps of problem solving, easily remembered with the fun pneumonic D.I.R.T.:

D = Define, as in define the problem

I = Identify, as in identify choices

R = Reflect, as in reflect on the choices

T = Try, as in try it out.

The idea is to help children brainstorm, when they are coolheaded, as many options as possible for approaching a given problem. Then the counselor can encourage them to work through their options mentally, choose one, and then try it out. The goal, through diligent practice and rehearsal, is to have these skills become second nature. D.I.R.T. can also be found on page 154 in Appendix C.

Define the Problem

The first step with children who are upset is to help them talk out their feelings and cool down. Sometimes it's helpful to assist them in performing relaxation exercises. Expressions of empathy and support from the counselor can also diffuse upset in children. The goal is to help them arrive at a point where the intensity of the feelings is no longer overwhelming and they feel back in control. As their level of arousal is lowered and their brains begin to reason, help them define the problem as specifically as possible.

Identify Choices

When children are ready, encourage them to use their "good brains" to identify options for approaching the problem. During the brainstorming, it's helpful if the counselor writes down the child's ideas. This exercise of writing down their thoughts gives validity and weight to their ideas.

Children should be encouraged to develop as comprehensive a list as possible and not reject or withhold any ideas initially. The counselor may contribute some ideas, too, but should be careful not to be overbearing or critical of any of the initial suggestions.

Reflect on the Choices

The next step would be to have children work through the list mentally, visualizing the likely outcome of each approach. After they have covered the list, they should be encouraged to pick the option that they think will result in the best outcome.

Try It Out

Finally, encourage them to try out their chosen option and report back to you regarding the results.

Many children who have ADHD behave aggressively. They act before thinking ahead to the consequences. The idea is to train them to become experts on slowing down and thinking before acting.

One excellent way to reinforce the concepts of problem solving is to role-play. You can hand out STOP signs to some kids and ask them to hold them up when they see a "hotheaded" response. Kids love the power inherent in holding a STOP sign, and they love to correct each other. When kids deliver a hotheaded response to a problem scenario during a role play, they are clowning it up and having fun so no offense is taken when others hold up their STOP signs.

You can also create a game with a set of cards that have sample problems, a set of reaction cards that say either "hotheaded" or "coolheaded," and a set of consequence cards that say "long-term" or "short-term." You can take turns if you're working individually with a child, or go around the table if working with a group. The first child draws a problem card and reads it out loud. The next child draws a reaction card (either hotheaded or coolheaded) and responds with a possible reaction to the problem card, one that fits in the proper category. Finally, the third child picks a consequence card (either long-term or short-term) and gives an example of what an immediate or longer term outcome might be, given the reaction stated by the previous child.

The following sample problems are suggested:

SAMPLE PROBLEMS FOR ROLE PLAY

The class bully was making fun of my best friend.	Another child stole my Game Boy.	My sister broke my Xbox.
I was accused of cheating, but I didn't.	My mother is always late to pick me up.	My friend told the whole school a secret of mine.
Another child stole my money.	Another child pushed me.	Another child butted in line.

These problems and more can be found on page 155 in Appendix C; reaction cards and consequence cards can be found on page 156. Counselors can photocopy, laminate, and cut out the cards in order to play the game. Round and round it goes. No amount of practice and role play is too much with this basic but important skill.

Three other important skills to cover with kids with explosive anger are assertiveness, conflict resolution, and the handling of teasing. These are covered in Chapter 3 on social skills. You can help these children realize that their needs, wants, and feelings are important, that it's not okay for others to mistreat them. But you can offer alternatives to blowing up when they feel slighted. The idea is to teach them effective and safe ways of expressing their anger and getting what they want. At the same time, you want to help them appreciate that aggression only generates more conflicts, gets people or property hurt, gets them in trouble, and usually does not get them what they sought in the first place.

Consider the following example:

Nolan was a disruptive child. With poor impulse control and difficulty interpreting social cues, he was chronically engaging in some form of classroom altercation. A simple example that occurred with predictable regularity was Nolan's pushing in line. Typically, Nolan's pushing-or-shoving behavior was in response to his perception that another child had intentionally pushed or shoved him. As a socially immature second-grader, Nolan interpreted his classmates' compet-itive "line up" behavior quite personally. He inevitably took offense if he was bumped or unintentionally pushed by another child as they scrambled to line up. A successful intervention occurred when the classroom participated in a role play.

He and his classmates were invited to participate in a role play in an effort to help Nolan develop more effective line behavior. As requested, the group got in a line and intentionally role-played— bumping, touching, and squeezing up against Nolan. Although the interaction was clearly simulated, Nolan's agitation quickly became apparent. A time-out was called, and Nolan was asked to consider how he was feeling. He admitted to feeling very angry. The group discussed how often they had felt wronged when others inadver-tently bumped or pushed them in line. They discussed ways to deal with those feelings—using words, rather than responding physi-cally. The role play was resumed and Nolan's reaction was signifi-cantly different. Rather than demonstrating his anger, he actually began to smile, betraying his recognition that the group was work-ing together to solve a common dilemma. The role play was stopped and again discussed. A third time the pushing-and-shoving line-up behavior was reenacted, and Nolan breezed through the appropriate response.

Six weeks later, his teacher reported that there had been no recur-rence of his violent temper in line (previously often a daily occur-rence) after the intervention.

CLASSROOM INTERVENTIONS FOR CHILDREN WITH ADHD

Strategies for Improving Attention

Teachers are advised to seat children with ADHD up front, close to them, and to provide one instruction at a time, repeat the instruction, and keep all instructions brief. Assignments should be broken up into bite-size workable steps, and the child with ADHD should be asked to repeat the instructions so as to demonstrate clear understanding. Written instructions should be given along with oral instructions, and visual aides should be employed whenever possible. The child with ADHD should be taught techniques for active reading, including underlining, highlighting, or taking notes. Remedial help may be needed to ensure success for the child with ADHD.

The ADHD or disruptive child responds best to a very structured classroom setting in which rules and expectations are clear, predictable, and known in advance. Also, children with ADHD learn better in spurts and cannot track well during long didactic lectures. Twelve 5-minute assignments achieve more with a child with ADHD than two 30-minute assignments. A child with ADHD is also helped by frequent breaks and can be invited to run errands or erase the chalkboard.

Strategies for Improving Compliance

All children, but particularly disruptive children, respond best to lots of positive reinforcement and reward for good behavior rather than scolding or punishments for negative behavior. Negative attention leads to more negative behavior, and many disruptive children seem to thrive or almost be addicted to negative attention from authority figures. These children are often experts on "pushing the buttons" of responsible adults and affecting a strong negative reaction from others. Teachers should be encouraged, if possible, to ignore low-level negative behavior. They should instead actively tune into and praise appropriate and desired behaviors as they appear. Any approximation of desirable behavior, particularly in a typically noncompliant or disruptive child, or any improvement in behavior should be acknowledged, praised, and rewarded. If a child complies with directions but exhibits a bad attitude, the compliance should be praised and the bad attitude ignored. Obviously, unsafe behavior cannot be ignored, but in addressing these behaviors, the teacher should attempt to retain as calm a demeanor and tone of voice as possible. A teacher becoming highly agitated leads to further arousal in an already out-of-control child. The teacher may find that by simply acknowledging the child's feelings and saying nurturing, supportive things in a soft, reassuring voice, he or she can de-escalate a situation and avert a meltdown in an agitated child.

Greene (2001) has conceptualized explosive, oppositional, socially impaired children as having skills deficits. He likens the underlying cause of their behavioral and social problems to a developmental delay or learning disability. These disruptive children simply haven't yet mastered reading social cues, resolving social conflict (in a healthy, productive way), regulating their affect, and problem solving. They "melt down" when faced with social conflict or when things don't go exactly according to their plan or expectations. With this as a conceptual framework, Greene recommends parents and teachers make every effort to modify the disruptive child's environment to increase the chances for social and academic success. He advises that the grown-ups make every effort to reduce demands on children with disruptive behavior disorders. Greene and his group at Harvard University are in the process of developing a school-based, cognitive-behavioral program for explosive children, modeled on Greene's earlier collaborative problem-solving approach for parents that is detailed in his book *The Explosive Child* (2001). This program has been empirically validated and has actually demonstrated superior efficacy over the well-established parent training program for oppositional children developed by Barkley (1997).

BEHAVIORAL CONTRACTS FOR THE CLASSROOM

Behavioral contracts are extremely helpful in disrupting a vicious cycle of negative behavior that begets negative attention that begets negative behavior. The idea is to create a way to turn the situation around and make it more positive, build up the self-esteem of an acting-out child, and teach that child how to get positive attention. The hope is that the teacher, counselor, parents, and children involved can work toward a common, prosocial goal where everyone feels like a winner.

There are essentially three major components to an effective behavioral contract: identified target behaviors, a tracking system, and a rewards menu. When developing a contract, it is important for the counselor to collaborate with the teachers, parents, and child. The idea is that if the stakeholders have input into the program, they are more likely to be invested and compliant.

Target Behaviors

When developing targets, it's important to be sure you are on target and identify the most problematic behaviors. Disruptive children tend to be off task, talk excessively, or be aggressive. It is also important to identify only a few (two or three) targets at a time, to carefully pick your battles, and to set up a program that is reasonable and achievable for the child. The targets should be very specific and worded affirmatively. I have seen many school contracts where a child receives a smiley face for "being good." However, these programs mean little to a child whose version of being good might be completely different from that of an adult. Any time children who are disruptive or oppositional are told "Don't," "No," or "You can't," they are likely to resist and defy the authority figure delivering the commands. So, rather than, "Don't hit," it is better to say, "Keep your hands and feet to yourself." Rather than, "No name-calling," it is better to say, "Refer to others by their given names at all times." Rather than, "Stop talking," it is better to say, "Speak only when it's your turn." If a child refuses to follow directions, you could phrase the target behavior, "Follow directions by the count of five."

Tracking

A key ingredient to a successful behavioral program is a diligently applied tracking system. For younger children, stickers work well. For older children, a system of tokens or points can be devised. The tracking system should be carefully and colorfully displayed as a constant reminder of how much success the child has achieved. A large calendar posted in an obvious place works well. The tracking system should have set times when stickers, points, or tokens are rewarded, denied, or deducted. For instance, points can be awarded at the end of each class period, or at three designated times throughout the day, say at 10 a.m., 12 noon, and 2 p.m. There should also be opportunities for bonus points. Behavioral psychology research shows that the most effective type of reward is intermittent positive reinforcement. This means that a target behavior is most likely to increase when rewards are given periodically, on an intermittent basis. This principle also applies with slot machines in Las Vegas, where players feel compelled to keep dropping coins because they occasionally get rewarded and they never know when they might hit the jackpot.

Deduction of points is a possible option for not meeting behavioral targets. However, when first implementing a program it is advisable to defer using this option. When a child is demoralized and accustomed to lots of negative attention and failures, the goal initially is to focus on changing the tone, reversing the behavioral–teacher response dynamics. The idea is to catch these children being good and reward and praise them regularly and often. The attitude when children fail to meet their targets should be matter of fact ("Oh well"), not overly critical or punitive. For many children, not making their targets and failing to earn points and teacher approval and praise is punishment enough, and overt criticism just leaves them feeling depleted and demoralized. Deductions can be added at some point, but only if that option is first negotiated with all parties as an addition to the contract. It is important that nothing is added as a surprise to the child because they will feel cheated and disempowered if the teacher or parent makes up rules on the spot.

Competition is a powerful reinforcer, so it is helpful to have several or all students competing for tokens, points, and rewards. It is also helpful to use the concepts of peer pressure and team spirit in behavioral contracts. In addition to working for themselves, a class goal for a reward all classmates will enjoy together is helpful.

Rewards Menu

In developing a rewards menu, it is useful to get input from the child. Sometimes, parents and teachers think they know what kids want, but they could be wrong. Having children help develop their own rewards menus increases the likelihood that they will buy into the program and strive to comply with it. Often, parents are recruited to purchase or arrange for the rewards. The rewards selected should be very specific— something in particular that the child is highly motivated to earn. The rewards can be material things, such as toys, games, or money, or things such as dinner at a favorite restaurant or a trip to the zoo. It's good to have options, with perhaps three different levels of awards, such as small, medium, and large, worth 50, 100, and 150 points, respectively. The child can choose to save up points for large rewards or turn them in early for small rewards. Having visual cues for the reward menu is helpful, such as a large poster that the child creates with pictures of possible rewards.

In addition to creating a large poster colorfully depicting potential rewards, construct a behavioral contract in writing. Successful behavioral contracts at school typically have approval from teachers, parents, and the students, and such contracts should be signed by all parties. Another feature of effective contracts is that they are kept simple—all parties are clear regarding the terms. Finally, it is helpful to acknowledge at the beginning that the contract may fail to result in modification of behavior and the contract may need to be modified and renegotiated.

Figures 7.1 and 7.2 show sample contracts for addressing typical disruptive behaviors. These can also be found on pages 158–160 in Appendix D, along with a calendar for tracking points to go along with the first behavioral contract.

STRATEGIES FOR IMPROVING ORGANIZATION AND PRODUCTIVITY

Teachers can help children with ADHD by frequently reminding them to slow down and double-check their work to reduce the rate of careless errors. Children with ADHD are typically disorganized and tend to lose things and forget things necessary for schoolwork. They can be taught to maintain daily checklists in a special notebook or day planner of homework assignments. Initially, especially, they are likely to need coaching in developing these types of organizational methods.

_____'s Behavioral Contract

Targets: 1. "I will speak only when it's my turn."
2. "I will follow directions by the count of 5."
3. "I will keep my hands and feet to myself."

Tracking: I will receive 1 point per target met at 10 a.m., 12 noon, and 2 p.m., for a possible total of 9 points per day.

My teacher will log the points into my log book and initial them three times per day.

I will review the log book with my parents each evening, and they will also track my points.

Rewards Menu: 50 Points = Get to order pizza for dinner
100 Points = Trip to bowling alley with Dad
150 Points = Game for Nintendo

FIGURE 7.1 SAMPLE BEHAVIORAL CONTRACT FOR HOME AND SCHOOL

_____'s Behavioral Contract

Targets: 1. Complete and turn in homework daily.
2. Complete and turn in classwork daily.
3. Attend all classes unless medically excused.

Tracking System:
1. _____must obtain signatures on day planner from all teachers whose classes were attended that day to verify classwork and homework completion and on-time submission. Teachers refuse to sign if homework or classwork not completed or turned in.
2. _____must provide parent(s) with class schedule so signatures of appropriate teachers can be verified.
3. Day planner with signatures shown to parent(s) daily.

Rewards System:
1. For each day student meets all three targets, may have usual privileges (e.g., TV, time with friends, playing outside).
2. When reaches 30 days of compliance, may earn special outing (e.g., zoo, bowling, movies, _____).
3. Each day fails to meet targets, confined to room, usual privileges revoked.

Signatures:

Parent_____

Student _____

Teacher _____

FIGURE 7.2   SAMPLE CONTRACT FOR THE HOMEWORK/SCHOOLWORK–NEGLIGENT CHILD

Teachers can also assist children with ADHD by dividing their worksheets into sections and reducing their amounts of homework. Math problems and written assignments especially may prove extremely difficult and time-consuming for children with ADHD, and reducing the quantity of these types of tasks is recommended. Another option teachers have is allowing extra time for children with ADHD to complete tests or in-school assignments. Following up with children with ADHD regarding incomplete or late assignments also increases their chances for success.

The Difficult Child: What to Do When You've Tried Everything

—by Kathy Weldon, MA

*S*ome children present with such chronic and severe academic, emotional, and behavioral problems that they leave us feeling overwhelmed and inadequate. Often they come to us with a history of having received a vast array of interventions and behavior management programs, yet somehow their behavior seems resistant to even the best laid plans. It is common for school staff and even parents to react with what psychiatrists call "negative countertransference." That is, these children tend to generate negative feelings in others, and school staff might feel inclined to push these children out and experience a wish that they would just go away. It's essential to monitor for these types of reactions and attempt to rally support for these children. It's helpful to approach these children in a compassionate, rather than rejecting, manner.

So, too, these children often have psychological defenses in place that cause them to alienate and push others away, so that they won't feel vulnerable and set themselves up for rejection. These children feel inadequate and demoralized, but often present as belligerent and prickly. It helps to constantly remind yourself, school staff, and parents that if these children could figure out a way to be accepted and successful, they would. We all want to be liked and to excel, but these kids just can't seem to find a formula for success in any arena of their lives.

Such children are well aware that they have problems. However, they may not understand what it is that they do that causes them to fail and be rejected. They often outwardly blame others. They may feel alienated, hurt, and even victimized, but deep down, they often feel that they are fundamentally defective or broken beyond repair.

Most people have a tendency to blame themselves when their lives are going poorly. Although not always consciously, those who are struggling might engage in a stream of self-deprecating commentary, such as, "I shouldn't have done that," "I'm so stupid," or "It's all my fault." Repeated failure can leave these children with anxiety, low self-confidence, and a sense of helplessness and even hopelessness.

Children with chronic school-related problems blame themselves in a very similar way. Although they are unlikely to admit to you that they blame themselves, and they tend to become defensive when confronted regarding their inappropriate behaviors, they secretly harbor enormous self-doubt and even self-loathing.

The problem with this deep sense of self-doubt and self-loathing is that it becomes a self-fulfilling prophecy. These children soon begin to expect social and academic failure, and they assume that others expect the same of them. We know well that in the educational environment, the latter often becomes the reality. Students with major problems get identified early and become the well-known "problem children" in the school, and teachers soon shudder at the sound of their names. Teachers, administrators, counselors, school psychologists, and other faculty personnel might all get pulled into consulting about these children. School staff tend to give up as a result of feeling ill-equipped to deal with these seemingly treatment-refractory children.

Fortunately, there are some effective techniques that can make a difference with these students. They involve a commitment to working with the students in individual or group counseling (with others of perhaps varying expressions of similar concerns). Initially, we suggest working with the students' teachers and parents to persuade them to abandon ineffective techniques that they are currently using. However, whether or not they are able to comply (not all adults are easily persuaded to give up their favorite modes of discipline), the bulk of your work with the difficult children will occur either in individual or group counseling sessions.

In this chapter we have outlined a direction for the process of counseling, and although we are typically referring to individual counseling, the same outline could easily (and sometimes more effectively) be adapted to a group setting. An essential step is to plan, schedule, and keep a series of counseling sessions, of 20–40 minutes, on a weekly or twice-weekly schedule for as many sessions as needed to produce the desired result (usually anywhere from 8–15 sessions). Less than 8 is probably too few with most difficult students, and more than 15 sessions may commit you to delve into a greater depth of therapy than you may feel qualified or comfortable to conduct.

Schedule and keep your appointments and listen. Don't be late and don't allow interruptions. These children are fragile and waiting to be rejected, with a tendency to interpret negative circumstances very personally.

LET GO OF TECHNIQUES THAT DO NOT WORK

What to do when nothing works? First off, it's essential to stop using the techniques that work so well with many students. These children are tough cases, and standard behavioral contracts do not work with them. We often hear that a difficult child has received a multitude of discipline slips (more than two in a given month is a multitude) or has missed recess for two consecutive weeks (three days is enough). In other words, if a normal discipline technique isn't working (and it's not working if the child is still behaving so that he or she is still getting the same consequence), then abandon the failed strategy.

In her parenting book *Positive Discipline,* Nelson (1987) describes the discouraged child as one who has an underlying goal of proving his or her inadequacy. She notes that even those behavior management skills (natural and logical consequences) that are typically effective are often proven ineffective with the discouraged child.

Even more disconcerting is the reality that many educators and adults often have a traditional authoritarian approach to discipline, where they view punishment as an essential ingredient in promoting compliant behavior. Even when a series of consequences or punishments have clearly had no positive impact on behavior, well-intended school staff may feel compelled to "serve up a little pain." Nelson comments on this tendency to apply negative punishments: "Where did we ever get the crazy idea that in order to make children do better, first we have to make them feel worse? Think of the last time you felt humiliated or treated unfairly. Did you feel like cooperating or doing better?"

Gerald was a fifth grader who had been banned from playing with a basketball for three consecutive semesters (18 weeks) in a row. His parents insisted on that particular consequence, knowing how much he loved to play, in an effort to motivate him to achieve better grades. By the time I saw Gerald, he reassured me that not only did he hate basketball and swore that he would never touch one again, but that he fully intended to continue failing in order to "show" his parents.

So the first important guideline in dealing with difficult children is being willing to let go of techniques that are not working. And the technique is not working if, after implementation, the child's behavior is unchanged or worse.

OFFER HOPE TO THE DISCOURAGED CHILD

It is essential that counselors do not become discouraged. Often, when our usual bag of tricks has failed, we are tempted to give up. If you are going to make a difference, you must be willing to accept the failure of a particular plan, go back to the drawing board, and come up with Plan B.

As stated earlier, children with chronic and severe behavior problems have given up on themselves, expect failure, and expect others to anticipate the same. A powerful and therapeutic intervention is simply your tenacious refusal to accept failure, which you repeatedly demonstrate to the child through words and deeds. You must reassure yourself and the difficult student that you will not give up until you have both found a formula that will enable the student to be successful and realize his or her potential.

It will not require a great deal of digging into the student's history and family environment to appreciate that everything has not always been up to par. Often these are students who will be referred for further evaluation, family counseling, or even child protective services. They may come from mildly or severely dysfunctional schools or home environments, in which they have experienced much disappointment and unpleasantness. Their demoralization and despair causes them to have little faith that their lives will ever be anything but chaotic and tenuous. Your expression of faith and hope in their future can provide a desperately needed lifeline.

In one-on-one counseling sessions, reassure discouraged students that you are willing to do whatever it takes to help them succeed. Assure them that you are quite confident that together you will find a way to improve their current situations.

LISTEN TO THEIR STORIES

Your third important task in dealing with children with chronic and severe behavior problems is to listen to their stories. Schedule a series of brief individual counseling sessions, three to six 30-minute sessions, over a period of three weeks. Remember—no interruptions, no tardiness. Be a rock, 100% reliable and available at the agreed-upon scheduled times. Tell students your goal is to listen to their views of the problems, to help understand why things keep going the way they seem to be going, and to work in alliance with them to develop a plan for things to change. The process of revealing their stories to you in and of itself can be tremendously healing and cathartic. Ask anyone who has participated in a 12-step program such as Alcoholics Anonymous:

There is something very therapeutic about hearing and telling personal stories. It helps, too, when you share personal things, maybe even things about which you are ashamed, and no one runs out of the room screaming or rejects or judges you in any way.

Emphasize that your goal is for things in their world to change, rather than that they themselves will be the only ones to change. Because difficult children already feel so badly about themselves, a suggestion that they need to change only reaffirms that poor self-image. These children tend to be exquisitely sensitive to rejection and can better tolerate a plan where they don't feel blamed or shamed in any way. You can let them know that they will not be expected to change in a fundamental way, but that their interactions with the world can be altered significantly for the better.

These children ultimately, at some level, know what troubles them the most. However, do not expect the answer to come after a simple "why" question. "Why do you get in trouble?" is a dead-end question, which leaves them feeling defensive and ashamed. Rather, ask them about their lives. What is going on in the classroom, what do they like and not like about school, and so on are leading questions that can point you to the heart of their problems.

Ask them to tell you about their lives, significant early experiences, and their hopes and disappointments. Utilizing an Adlerian-type questioning style (Stein, 1993), you might ask students to describe the significant people (family, friends, etc.) in their lives, allowing you to gain insight into their perception of their roles in the world. Ask them to describe early memories, as if they were looking at a scrapbook of their lives. Students can be encouraged to describe any early memories because the fact that something (an event in a moment in time) is frozen into their memory suggests, according to Adler (1933), that that event or moment was significant in their view of themselves or the world.

The important part of this phase of intervention is to get the student talking. Having laid a foundation of hope, you must now begin to understand the emotional and psychological contexts in which the student has been living. Only they can help you uncover their views of themselves, others, and the world, because their perspectives are specifically guided by their personal beliefs and assumptions. Any experienced counselor will reassure you, "If you ask, they will tell you." It is a basic assumption in counseling and psychotherapy that the clients are just dying to tell you their stories.

Consider the following example:

Randall was just such a student as previously described. He was chronically unhappy, emotionally volatile, and quick to blow up with teachers and peers. With a history dating back to first grade, Randall was always getting in trouble with his teachers or creating conflict among his classmates. Lacking social skills, he continually generated rejection. By the time the counselor began working with Randall, he had had five miserable years of social torment.

Randall no longer believed that he could possibly be likeable, and predictably, his behavior fell in step with his belief. He annoyed, agitated, and appalled his classmates and was continually the victim of teasing. He was eventually diagnosed as clinically depressed, and his parents were persuaded to seek treatment for his depression, but in the interim, the school had to work with Randall.

Typically, the counselor was summoned to retrieve him when he had lost control. He might be under his desk, rocking and crying, or banging his head saying statements such as, "I'm so stupid." Interestingly, Randall was not stupid at all, but actually quite gifted. He participated in the gifted program, but clearly, this did little to challenge his sense of low self-worth.

After working with Randall on several occasions, the counselor realized that traditional strategies were of no avail. Telling him he was smart, attractive, likeable, or anything positive was like trying to mix oil and water. Acknowledgments had no effect. It soon became clear that Randall's issues were much deeper. His deep sense of self-loathing would have to be confronted.

It is difficult to challenge someone's core beliefs about himself or herself by directly confronting that belief. As already mentioned, praise and acknowledgment have little lasting effect. As in Randall's case, even positive experiences don't seem to impact or alter the core issues. The fact that he was gifted seemed superfluous because he tenaciously clung to a wretched sense of self-worth. Regardless of the circumstances, Randall felt that he was inherently "wrong" because he viewed himself as fundamentally defective and broken beyond repair.

Over a period of several weeks, Randall began to tell his story to the counselor. With memories beginning in the first grade and continuing throughout his fifth year of school, Randall was clearly demoralized and felt hopeless regarding any potential that he would ever become a successful and accepted student and peer.

IDENTIFY THEMES AND PATTERNS IN THE STUDENT'S STORIES

Identifying a pattern in an individual's stories is usually not a difficult task. Over the course of many hours of individual counseling with children and adults, we have found that almost all individuals have memories of specific events or moments in time when they felt particularly small, inept, ashamed, not good enough, unloved, unwanted, or some other variation of a theme of inadequacy. By listening to the student's stories, the counselor will notice how particular situations might have held negative meanings.

Often, when hearing a story, we might ask, "What did you feel at that moment?" or "How did that make you feel about yourself?" It is often useful to look for the specific impact of a significant event. For example, after listening to a student recant a moment when her mother had caught her stealing from a store, the counselor asked her, "What did you think that meant about yourself?" After a brief silence, the student replied, "I was bad."

We all have a tendency to cling to significant, emotional memories, which generated for us particular core beliefs about ourselves and the world. It is as though an event is recorded in our minds (not always accurately, by the way, but subject to one's personal interpretations), and then we form a conclusion about the underlying meaning(s) of that event, which then becomes part of our core belief system.

James recalled a memory when he was unable to accomplish a task, which appeared to come easily to his older siblings. With prompting, he acknowledged that he harbored a feeling of inadequacy as he recalled that experience. A similar theme of inadequacy emerged in another memory he shared (being unable to read as well as peers in a first-grade reading group), indicating that he had generated a general conclusion about himself: that he was inadequate when compared with others.

CONFRONT THE UNDERLYING BELIEF

After noting a particular pattern or theme, the counselor can gently suggest to students that they may have developed a belief about themselves. Typically, especially when a strong rapport or alliance has been built up, students can quickly identify and acknowledge that they do indeed feel inadequate, or whatever the underlying feeling may be. Students often experience tremendous relief at this point, simply because they finally feel understood and accepted by a person (you) that they have grown to admire and respect. At last someone is on their side, seeing things from their perspectives. They may have even come to believe and trust that you actually really like them and care about them. What a revelation that can be for some children.

Your next job is to help students confront the rationality of their beliefs. This is not always an easy task. Let's take the example of Megan, who recognized that she felt that she was fundamentally "bad" after recounting several early memories, including the one already described when her mother had caught her stealing. Megan was constantly trying to avoid attention from adults and peers, fearful that they, too, would recognize that she was indeed a bad girl. Although she did not manifest overt behavioral problems, Megan was so unsure of herself that she produced no work for her teacher and was failing her fifth-grade classes. Megan's current experience of academic failure only added further proof, in her mind, that she was indeed bad (fulfilling her private prophecy of personal failure).

She was asked to reconsider her early memories and revisit the conclusion that she had drawn from those early experiences. Was it really true that she was a bad girl because she had wanted to take something from the grocery store? Had she really been guilty of theft? Should her character be considered profoundly defective because at the tender age of four she had lacked the discretion to not steal?

After gently guiding her to acknowledge that her early conclusion may have been a bit harsh, the counselor's next step was to point out that this underlying belief continued to instruct her current behavior. Megan was confronted with the likelihood that her avoidance of schoolwork was an effort to avoid a task in which she might do poorly or further demonstrate her "badness." Megan was psychologically paralyzed; she avoided activities in which she might be evaluated, assured that she would fail. And naturally, her avoidance of activities ensured that she would continue on a path of personal failure.

Persuading an individual that current behavior is guided by distorted and flawed early beliefs may not be easy. Having constructed a paradigm of self that is created around a belief of personal inadequacy, humans are inevitably constrained in their abilities to see around that personal paradigm. They tend to filter out evidence that contradicts their core beliefs and focus instead on evidence that promotes these beliefs.

An effective technique to help a child get started with the process of recontouring personal paradigms is to revisit a well-known history lesson. One example is that there was a point in time when the general population considered the earth to be flat. This conclusion was embraced by the current worldview or world paradigm and generally went unquestioned by thousands of individuals. Their experience of the world inevitably seemed to support this accepted conclusion. To not question the validity of this paradigm, individuals had to repeatedly ignore evidence that the world was round (for example, the experience of things such as ships moving away and disappearing below the horizon only to find them returning having failed to fall off the edge of the earth).

When popular opinion reconcluded that the world was indeed round, the general population was able to effectively ignore all evidence that suggested that the world might be flat. The fact is, the cognitive paradigm or perceptual filter by which people live governs the way they interpret their experiences. Experience does not dictate one's reality, but rather one's paradigm dictates one's interpretation and experience of "reality."

Having a student realize that his or her current experience is governed by a paradigm or belief about him- or herself or the world, which is founded on early irrational conclusions, is not easy, but it can be a monumental achievement in the process of working with the severely and chronically demoralized student.

Returning to Randall for a moment:

After hearing his stories, it became clear that Randall felt as though he was not good enough to be accepted by his teachers and peers. Upon confrontation that he had embraced this belief, Randall at first became defensive and adamantly denied this belief. However, as the counselor gently outlined the pattern that had emerged as he had presented in his stories (a significant reprimand by his first-grade teacher, teasing by second-grade peers, bullied in third grade, and the list went on), Randall could not help but recognize and acknowledge his enormous self-doubt and even self-loathing.

In many of Randall's early recollections, he had presented themes of rejection. By repeating his stories back to him, exactly as he had told them, the counselor was able to help Randall recognize the theme. And having acknowledged a theme, Randall was able to articulate a hidden but profound belief that he embraced about himself. Randall was somehow "wrong." He was unacceptable, unlovable, and clearly lacking in some vital ingredient that would otherwise make him acceptable to the majority of the human race. Randall was broken beyond repair in his own mind (and in his interpretation of the reactions of others).

When confronted over a period of several sessions with the reality that his early conclusions were irrational and invalid, and that these flawed beliefs had been governing his experiences, Randall expressed an intense sense of relief. Releasing a long sigh and with an expression of profound realization, Randall exclaimed, "I'm not really wrong! None of these things really means anything about myself, unless I tell myself that it means I'm bad!" Randall had made a very significant step toward personal change.

ASSIST THE STUDENT TO ABANDON SELF-JUDGMENT

As illustrated earlier, world and personal paradigms might seem resistant to change, but after they are challenged, they can often be modified. Nevertheless, even after the old paradigm is successfully challenged, an individual needs tools for constructing a new, more positive (and realistic) paradigm of self and the world. Because students realize they have acted under an irrational view of self does not guarantee that they will immediately change their behavior to conform to a new view of self. And to avoid the risk that any new negative experiences will cause them to think again, "Maybe my earlier conclusion was indeed correct," it is important to create a different context for interpreting experience.

To create a context for a new and improved paradigm, it is imperative to help rid students of damaging patterns of self-judgment.

An effective activity is one called "tearing up my personal report card." We first ask students to list on a sheet of paper all their strengths, or their good and positive attributes. We then ask them to turn over the paper and list all their weaknesses, or their bad and negative attributes. Depending on the particular student (and this activity can be useful with all students, not just the severely discouraged), some will have a lot more to list on the back side than on the front.

We then describe this paper as a self-administered report card, which they all carry with them constantly (metaphorically speaking). We ask each student to consider how he or she feels about this report card.

For those students with the longer negative list, we then question whether or not it is a good idea to carry something around with us, all day, every day, that makes us feel badly about ourselves. We then ask the students to consider what it would be like if neither the front nor the back side of this report card contained any valid information: "What if, in fact, there is no truth that this or that is good or bad about you? What if these are simply things that you do or don't do, but they really don't mean anything about who you are personally? In other words, what if you were no longer allowed to grade or evaluate your own behavior? What if you simply described yourself as being able to read well but that didn't mean you were in any way 'good'? Or if you described yourself as someone that makes your teacher yell, but that doesn't mean that you are in any way 'bad'? What if you simply described your behaviors as behaviors and don't use them to formulate labels about who you are as a person?"

We then ask students to tear up their personal report card and try to view their behavior as simply behaviors that mean virtually nothing with regard to their personhood and underlying worth. We ask students to consider the possibility that there are neither "good" nor "bad" people, but instead that all human beings are able to act in a wide variety of ways, some effective and some not so effective. This phrase leads us to the final phase of our counseling intervention, but it is important to note that at this point most students express a profound sense of relief and personal freedom. They inevitably relish the possibility of living in a world where they are not continually judging themselves, or being judged by others.

GENERATE BEHAVIORAL GOALS AND A PLAN TO SUPPORT THOSE GOALS

The final phase of counseling severely discouraged students involves creating a new paradigm in which they can interpret their experiences. Having confronted their irrational view of self and further challenged their tendency to interpret their ongoing experiences and behaviors through a filter of self-judgment, it is time to give them some powerful tools for changing their behavior.

These tools, although very similar to traditional behavior goals, are intrinsically unique because of the context in which they are created. Traditional behavioral goals work within the paradigm that there is something "wrong" with the student and that that thing needs to be changed. The following behavioral goals work within a paradigm in which nothing is inherently wrong with the student, just that some behaviors tend to be more effective than others. Although the distinction may seem trivial, it is vital to developing an effective intervention with a severely discouraged child.

Remember that severely discouraged children have given up on themselves, concluding that they are incapable of change. Having confronted the underlying self-defeating beliefs and challenged ongoing tendencies for self-judgment, discouraged individuals must be convinced of their need to change their behaviors to realize personal goals.

Together we identify personal goals. It is essential that the spirit of the approach to developing a behavioral contract is one of collaboration and negotiation. You communicate clearly the messages, "We're all in this together and we're all on the same side" and "We need to work together to be successful." Behavioral contracts developed without input from the children themselves are likely to fail. The students must feel they are part of the process, they have a voice, and their opinions, feelings, and thoughts are valued and respected. Involving students in the process is an essential mechanism for achieving their investment in the effort. Even the most discouraged student will quickly identify goals that are common to all human beings, such as "to be accepted and loved," "to have friends," "to please others (teachers, parents, etc.)," "to be happy," and so on. As soon as goals are agreed upon, we then discuss behaviors in the context of their effectiveness or ineffectiveness in helping students realize these goals. Students are often excited and feel empowered by this fresh way of discussing behaviors. They can easily identify behaviors that help them and behaviors that defeat their identified goals.

At this final stage, it is usually an easy sell to create behavioral contracts that help students work on behaviors that carry them forward, toward their goals of feeling loved and accepted. Having shed the burden of a foregone conclusion of personal failure, they often express a sense of renewed energy and power to behave in ways that had previously seemed beyond their reach. As they begin to act in new ways, the world around them begins to validate the effectiveness of their new behaviors by responding and reacting to them in new ways, creating a new and more positive self-fulfilling paradigm.

Working With Groups or Classes: How to Intervene With More Than One Child

—by Kathy Weldon, MA

*W*orking with students in counseling groups or classroom interventions is often the therapeutic modality of choice. Timewise, it is more efficient, but there are other important advantages as well. There are also certain situations where group counseling or classroom interventions would be ill-advised. In this chapter we will provide some general group counseling guidelines and classroom intervention guidelines. We will also provide some specific group formats and classroom activities that can be easily implemented. But before we address the specifics of group and classroom interventions, let's consider the benefits of these modalities against some risks.

BENEFITS OF GROUP AND CLASSROOM INTERVENTIONS

Time Efficiency: Group or classroom interventions allow you to reach the greatest number of students in the least amount of time.

Least Restrictive: Group interventions are less restrictive than individual interventions, and of course, classroom interventions are considered the least restrictive option. Although parental permission is required for any intervention that removes the student from the classroom, such as in a counseling group, it may not be required for a classroom intervention (depending on the school policy). The reason, of course, is that classroom interventions are provided to all students equally and might be considered part of the school or grade curriculum.

Universality: Universality refers to the individual's experience that he or she is not alone in the universe. Students have the opportunity to realize that they are not the only ones feeling the way they do or experiencing things the way they are. For example, children dealing with their parents' divorce often benefit from realizing that other children are feeling the same loss, confusion, and sense of being overwhelmed.

Modeling: An important benefit in group and classroom interventions is that students have the opportunity to learn and model their behavior through observing their peers as they learn and gain insight. For example, in counseling groups of students suffering from high levels of anxiety, the participants were not only amazed to realize that other students felt as they did (universality), but very interested in hearing about how others were learning to cope with their anxiety.

Social Interactions: Group and classroom activities provide the opportunity for students to practice prosocial skills. This is particularly essential if you are addressing social skills concerns; students will benefit much more readily when they can immediately utilize and practice a skill they are discussing. The group or classroom environment also provides the opportunity for the facilitator to observe a student's level of prosocial behavior.

RISKS OF GROUP AND CLASSROOM INTERVENTIONS

Potential for Rejection: Certain problems, if addressed publicly, are likely to repulse peers. As an extreme example, bed-wetting would be a humiliating problem to address in a group or classroom situation. Other, less embarrassing problems might also generate rejection (e.g., theft, eating disorders) and should not be addressed in a classroom and only rarely, under specific circumstances, in a group. At the end of this chapter, we will provide a list of concerns that are appropriate for each modality (i.e., individual interventions, group interventions, and classroom interventions). It is strongly suggested that you not only refer to this list but consider the needs of each individual student (discuss with parent and teacher, etc.), prior to deciding to place a given child in a particular therapeutic modality.

Potential for Negative Learning: Certain negative behaviors can be learned in a group or classroom situation. Research by Chamberlain & Mihalic (1998) and others indicates that it can be counterproductive to facilitate a group of conduct-disordered youth. In fact, work by her group demonstrated that the amount of time spent with other conduct-disordered peers was the strongest risk factor in predicting recidivism. The risk of potential negative learning outweighs the potential benefits in this population.

NUTS AND BOLTS OF GROUP INTERVENTIONS

Behavior Management

A major concern in conducting groups with children is behavior management during the session. There is no value in trying to facilitate a counseling group with students who are behaviorally out of control, and behavior management is not always as easy as it might appear. It is important to take some time to formulate the behavioral expectations you have for your students and to create a plan for communicating those expectations. Finally, it is helpful to develop a plan of action to generate cooperation for your behavioral expectations.

Children often feel it is a privilege to participate in group counseling programs; they often enjoy the break from daily academic demands. The change in their ordinary routine and the novelty of sharing information that is not a part of their normal academic curriculum can be rewarding enough to motivate many children to be well behaved and cooperative. This type of reinforcement—simply the opportunity to participate—would be termed an "intrinsic reward" and is an inherent feature built into the group. Experience shows only rare occasions where students' behavior was so disruptive that they were dismissed from a particular group session, and inevitably those students made valiant efforts to avoid dismissal in following sessions. Often, peers or friends of group members will beg to be included in subsequent groups, whether they need it or not. Group participants often couldn't help but brag to friends regarding their selection and participation in a group. They typically perceived that they were special and fortunate to belong to a therapy group.

Nevertheless, it is often desirable to design a behavioral management program that offers some extrinsic incentives to stay on task, particularly for those students who may have a history of disruptive behavior. A nice program that was successfully utilized by the authors consists of a mixture of guidelines or target behaviors (better to avoid the term "rules," which connotes authoritarianism), established at the outset by the group members themselves and reiterated at each meeting, a tracking system for monitoring adherence to the guidelines, and a reward system. A sample program is outlined as follows:

Behavioral Program

Targets:
1. "I will speak only when it's my turn."
2. "I will follow directions by the count of 5."
3. "I will keep my hands and feet to myself."

Tracking:
  1. Each child will have three stars next to his or her name on a dry erase board.
  2. Each child who fails to meet a target will lose a star.

Consequences/Rewards:
  1. One star lost is considered a warning, and that child can still earn a prize.
  2. Two stars lost results in failure to earn a prize this session, but the child can remain in group and earn a rain check for next session to redeem the prize, if he or she keeps all three stars in the next session.
  3. Three stars (or strikes) lost and "You're outta here."
  4. Prizes are one item from prize basket per week.
  5. Each child is allowed to spend only 15 seconds selecting a prize.

As already noted, many children will be very motivated to follow the rules and cooperate with group expectations simply to maintain the privilege of attendance. However, some students have more difficulty because of their limited ability to control impulsive behaviors. These students can benefit from a behavior management plan.

It is important to keep behavior expectations simple and clear: Keep the number of rules to a minimum—say, no more than three. It is helpful to word the targets positively, in the affirmative, with emphasis on what *to do* rather than negatively with emphasis on what *not to do*. Also, careful and consistent tracking is a key ingredient to any effective behavior contract. The kids will be more compliant if they know they are being carefully monitored. Counselors may find that rewards have a high valence for the children, even if they are just small toys purchased at a dollar store. In one group, the rewards had such high valence that most kids said that they were the best part of the group meetings. In addition, many friends of the group members stopped by the clinic asking if they might be included in the groups so that they too might obtain prizes.

PLANNING COUNSELING GROUPS

Identify Population Needs

A variety of mental health concerns can be addressed in a group setting, depending on your population and their needs. It might be useful to survey teachers, counselors, administrators, and parents (or any one of those groups) early in the year and solicit their specific concerns and desires for services. A recent survey by our counseling staff indicated an immediate need for the following types of issues to be addressed:

- *Social skills training:* Typically, this is at the top of the list.
- *Prepuberty concerns:* Because of early development, lack of information, and sometimes inappropriate sexual comments, it was noted that many fifth-grade males and females might benefit from a group setting where they could safely and with the help of a guidance counselor address the changes they were beginning to experience.
- *Dealing with military deployments:* This is an issue specific to our community, where many children struggle with the difficulties associated with extended deployments of one or both parents.
- *Coping with anxiety:* Help dealing with anxiety is often requested by school staff in response to specific observations of students with tendencies to worry, be overly sensitive, or experience performance anxiety.
- *Fostering responsibility:* Typically, there is an ongoing need for help for those students who never complete work, never turn in homework assignments, arrive late, and so on.

All the issues in the preceding list would lend themselves to a group format.

It is not recommended that counselors select a group name according to the need it specifically addresses. For example, a divorce group might be called "New Beginnings" or "Changing Families," rather than "Divorce Group," which obviously has negative connotations. An anxiety group might be called "Feeling Free," or "Hakuna Matata," or "Cool Cats." Create a name for the group that subtly suggests its nature but has a positive or at least benign connotation to those who might want to participate.

Identifying Student Needs

Typically, a student is referred to a counselor by his teacher or parent because of specific behavioral or emotional concerns. As soon as possible, meet with the teachers and parents to obtain an accurate and detailed picture of what is going on with the student. Plan a classroom or playground observation, or both. Sometimes it is helpful to administer an informal screening instrument such as the Revised Children's Manifest Anxiety Scale (RCMAS; Reynolds & Richmond, 1978), which screens for anxiety, the Children's Depression Inventory (CDI; Kovacs, 1985), which screens for depression, or the BarOn EQ-I (Bar-On, 1997), which yields an emotional quotient correlated with mental health and adaptability. These paper-and-pencil instruments are quick and easy to administer, available to the public commercially, and can offer insight on the specific issues and severity of these issues involved with a particular student.

Perhaps the need for a specific group already has been identified because several students have presented who grapple with similar concerns. In an effort to develop a full group of, say, 5 to 8 participants, a letter can be circulated to the entire school staff requesting referrals for a planned group intervention. As the names are submitted, then each student is evaluated by the group facilitators as to his or her appropriateness for a particular group.

Obtaining Parent Permission

Obtaining parent permission for a son or daughter to attend a counseling group is not always an easy matter. Many parents fear exposure, and therefore hesitate or resist the idea. They worry that their child will speak too openly about home life and family. This is a common and normal reaction that often requires simple reassurances, such as, "Our group will follow a specific outline," or "The group will focus on sharing concerns that are relevant to the whole group and school setting."

You may need to "sell" your group to the parents of each student whom you invite to participate. Outline the benefits of group participation, as discussed earlier in this chapter. Additionally, some parents are reluctant to allow their children time away from academic instruction. In these cases, parents may need persuasion to understand that students whose mental health or well-being are compromised are less likely to succeed in school. In the long run, participation in the group is likely to result in enhanced academic performance among its participants.

GROUP PROCESSING

Almost any counseling group benefits from the opportunity to share and process information *as a group*. Group processing allows the individuals in the group to share their own perspectives and to understand and assimilate the perspectives of their peers on similar matters. This opportunity to share and discuss experiences provides an opportunity to increase capacity for social empathy and compassionate understanding, and to experience and learn more sophisticated problem-solving techniques. In particular, there is an opportunity to learn effective techniques for resolving social conflict. Additionally, group processing allows individuals to confront their own cognitive distortions about themselves and the world, as the group often provides a "reality check" for irrational thoughts and ideas.

Typically, members of the group are invited to share anything that they are comfortable sharing with their friends, but they are cautioned not to share anything that they feel is too personal or that might be embarrassing. The group is instructed to listen and accept each person's perspective and to not judge one another. The group is also asked to keep each other's confidences. However, because this request is not always honored—especially by children—the group is again reminded to discuss only things that they are comfortable sharing with their friends in general.

We have found that it is better to caution students to censor their own sharing, rather than encouraging them to share openly. Typically, if there is something that a student feels compelled to share, and the group has proved itself cohesive and trustworthy, then the student will share accordingly. However, if the group is not mature enough to handle a particular student's concerns in a respectful, nonjudgmental manner, then it is better that these concerns not be shared in a group format.

Finally, an important part of group processing is allowing the participants to discuss and offer solutions or other perspectives to an individual's experiences, thoughts, or both. The group facilitator should carefully monitor all feedback, reminding group members that it is important to maintain a safe, supportive, nonjudgmental environment. Following the rule of "no interruptions" after an individual shares, the facilitator may ask the individual who shared if he or she would like feedback from the group. If desired, the facilitator can invite feedback. If a peer begins to offer feedback that is harsh or judgmental, the facilitator may have to intervene and caution against further such feedback. In my experience, such events are actually quite rare—most peers seem to try their best to be supportive and helpful. Peers may not always offer the best of solutions or perspectives, but that's fine, as long as their feedback is not damaging to the individual who did the sharing. Feedback can be processed and discussed by the group to further highlight that everyone has different perspectives and ideas, even in response to the same event. The goal of group processing is simply to generate a lot of different perspectives and ideas about any one concern. The more an individual begins to realize that there are multiple perspectives and multiple solutions (regardless of how relevant or appropriate each is), the more likely he or she will feel that there is a possibility of looking at things differently. Likewise, the capacity for empathy toward others who are different is fostered and ideally experienced by the group.

A SAMPLE GROUP FORMAT – ANXIETY GROUP

In conducting any type of group counseling, it is typically best to start with a specific format or agenda and then allow deviation according to the needs and desires of individual students. There are many wonderful resources for group counseling activities available commercially, so we are simply providing a sample outline format for conducting a group that addresses anxiety. Research suggests that group therapy may be more effective than individual therapy in intervening with children with anxiety disorders.

Anxiety groups are helpful for those students who seem to be overly sensitive, worriers, anxious, or suffering from performance anxiety. An outline for a six-session anxiety group might look something like the following.

Session 1: Anxiety Versus Feelings of Ease

Define and discuss anxiety. As a group, brainstorm symptoms of anxiety (e.g., nervous, hypervigilance or being on-guard, sweaty palms, butterflies in stomach, feeling hot, turning red, etc.). Have students list situations in which they experience anxiety (e.g., speaking in public, taking a test, getting a report card, being in trouble with their parents, etc.) and situations in which they feel completely at ease. Make a good long list of many sample situations. Have students rate on a scale of 1–10 which situations are most and least anxiety producing.

Session 2: A Little Anxiety Is Good. . . Too Much Is Not

Discuss the performance–anxiety curve and its relationship to productivity. This curve appears below and is easy to reproduce on a chart or dry erase board.

Performance–Anxiety Curve

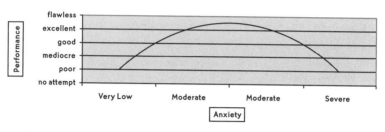

You can make the point that when we are alert and attentive (low anxiety), we tend to be effective, productive individuals; when we are too anxious, our effectiveness and productivity declines. So, too, it is helpful to point out that some anxiety is normal and adaptive. The goal is to contrast good and normal anxiety versus incapacitating, overwhelming anxiety. You can remark that only dead people have no anxiety. We need some anxiety to help us get up in the morning and do the things we need to do. Without *some* anxiety, we wouldn't function well or accomplish anything. So the point is that moderate anxiety enhances performance. Likewise, have students identify ways in which too much anxiety makes them less productive (e.g., become overly timid when asked to respond in class, do poorly on a math exam even though the material was understood the night before, etc.). They will likely easily recall experiences during which their anxiety soared and caused them to melt down and feel as if their brains had shut off.

Session 3: What Does Not Work to Reduce Anxiety?

What does not work to reduce anxiety? Have the group first address things that don't seem to help them feel more at ease and less anxious. Students might think of things they have been told to do in the past (e.g., "Don't worry!") or things they have tried without success (avoidance by distraction). Discuss why these efforts really do not work. For example, when a parent or older sibling tells you, "Don't worry— you're being silly," does that usually make you feel better? Or perhaps you are worried about a test, so you play video games the evening before. Does that help you feel less anxious about the test in the morning? Help students identify the things they are doing (e.g., overeating, watching too much TV, worrying, etc.) and how these not only do not help but may worsen anxiety. Generate a beginning list of things that do work to reduce anxiety.

Session 4: What Works to Reduce Anxiety?

Generate a list of things that students can do to reduce anxiety (e.g., exercise, relaxation, visualization, etc.). Spend the remainder of the group practicing one or more of these psychophysiological techniques for reducing anxiety. You can show them that by simply taking slow, deep breaths they can lower their arousal and more efficiently oxygenate their bodies. Relaxing the body relaxes the mind, and the brain can start functioning again. Let them know that mastering relaxation techniques will be difficult at first, especially for someone with chronic anxiety. Attempting to relax will feel unnatural to some, but with persistence even the most anxious child can learn relaxation skills. You should encourage the children to practice relaxation every day, at a set time—to work it into their daily routines, just like brushing their teeth. Practicing 15 minutes each night before bed is a helpful guideline. If they practice daily, they will lower their baseline level of anxiety, and after relaxation is mastered, they can adeptly deploy these techniques to get control when faced with a particular anxiety-provoking situation, such as a public performance or major exam. Many scripts for relaxation exercises are commercially available. Some sample scripts are included in Chapter 4, "The Anxious Child," as well as in Appendix B.

Session 5: Changing Your Thinking

Ideally, to reduce anxiety, an individual must think differently about the situation that is producing the anxiety. Introduce the notion of cognitive distortions—how individuals distort or misinterpret particular situations—and the consequences of those misrepresentations. Begin to confront the fact that events may not really have the impact that is often imagined and therefore fuels the high levels of anxiety. Use examples of phobias (that no one in the group shares) to illustrate the irrationality of that fear (e.g., fear of heights, spiders, flying, etc.). Have students discuss their own irrational thinking that causes them to experience unnecessary anxiety in their own lives. Discuss alternative ways to think about these situations.

Session 6: Review and Process

Summarize lessons from the group, and identify your own symptoms of anxiety. Notice how anxiety makes you less effective or productive in a given situation. Recognize what does not work to reduce anxiety, and identify some techniques that do work to reduce anxiety. Change irrational thinking about situations that produce anxiety, but acknowledge and discuss that life will always present us with anxiety-producing situations. It is most important to be equipped with ways to deal effectively and productively with those situations.

Additional interventions from Chapter 4, "The Anxious Child," can be adapted easily into a group format for working with a group of anxious children.

Consider the following example:

Sally, who was mentioned earlier (in the chapter on the depressed child) was extremely upset after spilling water on her pants and later refused to return to group. An intervention that was very cathartic for Sally was to first insist that she continue coming to the group. The next session was devoted to sharing embarrassing past experiences. Before starting this exercise, the group was reminded that for the group to be helpful, it had to remain a "safe" place. That meant that group members needed to protect each other's confidentiality. "Remember that what is said in here, stays in here." Group members were also reminded that they needed to be sensitive toward each other's feelings and be respectful and supportive of one another. As one group member shared an example of an embarrassing experience, other group members were invited to share their reactions. Also, group members were invited to share what they would say to reassure a best friend who had had such an embarrassing experience.

Generally, the group revealed that although people might feel embarrassed if they make a mistake publicly or spill something or trip, others don't rush to judge. Most of us are pretty good about forgiving others' imperfections and mistakes. It turned out no one had paid any attention to Sally spilling water on herself and certainly no one had reacted with a harsh judgment. Sally's perceptions in regard to others' reactions were flawed, and after she first had her feelings validated, it was helpful for her to hear the actual reactions of others, which were benign and accepting.

Another intervention that would have been helpful for Sally would have been to arrange for another child to spill water on himself at the beginning of the next group. Then the group could have had their attention drawn to the spill and asked for their reactions and thoughts. The group would have likely responded that they felt bad for the child who spilled water and that it could have happened to them. It is very unlikely that anyone in the group would have made a derogatory comment or passed judgment on the child who spilled water because even children understand that accidents happen and some things just can't be helped.

FINAL NOTE ON ROLE PLAYING

Role playing is one of the most effective venues for children to experience and explore the potential for change. As a normal part of child growth and development, children enjoy role-playing games. They relish the opportunity to try on different roles and will inevitably experience others' perspectives as a natural part of the process. As with Sally, observing another student role-play her experience would have offered her the opportunity to revise her perception of her own situation.

We have already referred to the use of role playing in other chapters because we see it as such a vital tool in working with groups of children. Regardless of the format and particular emphasis of the group, there are invariably opportunities to utilize role-playing activities. Students can be encouraged to try a new behavior to handle anxiety, to act out comebacks to put-downs, to practice prosocial behavior, to handle anger, and to develop a limitless number of other skills. Role plays afford the opportunity for them to experientially gain personal insight, empathy, and to practice needed skills in relevant areas of concern.

Crisis Intervention: How to Intervene in the Face of a Tragedy

—by Kathy Weldon, MA

*M*anaging crisis situations is a growing concern for school counselors. Until relatively recently, crises in the school setting often went completely ignored. Today, we recognize that not only are we at high risk of enduring a crisis in our schools at some point, but also that it is incumbent upon us to have an organized and prepared response to handle the crisis.

When traumatic events are poorly handled, there is potential for long-term fallout and dysfunction. An example of a crisis may be the untimely death of a teacher, suicide of a student, act of violence on school grounds, or a critical incident that occurs in the community, such as a natural disaster or act of terrorism. Many tools are available that offer guidance for specific crisis scenarios, so this is in no way intended to be a comprehensive discussion of the subject. Nevertheless, as it is likely that most school counselors will be faced with a crisis situation, we felt compelled to offer some brief but helpful guidelines.

Given the recent school-based tragedies, most schools have become well aware of the need for a general crisis response plan. Typically, a school- or district-wide response plan has been developed, with the specific needs of a particular population and community in mind. Ideally, this plan provides for an organized crisis response team, a way to assemble faculty, parents, and community members to disseminate information and resources. These guidelines were developed under the assumption that your school has already organized a crisis response plan specific to your needs. The intention here is simply to provide some overall principals for appropriate and effective crisis response intervention.

IMPORTANT CONSIDERATIONS IN CRISIS RESPONSE

Following are some important considerations, adapted from a survey of the effectiveness of early interventions for victims and survivors of mass violence, undertaken in a workshop format and published by the National Institute of Mental Health (NIMH) (2002).

It is inappropriate to presume that individuals will experience traumatic distress or clinically significant disorders as an inevitable reaction to a critical incident. Although it is essential to plan for immediate crisis response and psychological interventions, mental health care providers should expect normal recovery. The expectation of maladaptive response can inappropriately influence the planning and implementation of interventions.

Although large-scale group and individual interventions (counseling, debriefings, etc.) for survivors of mass violence can be beneficial, participation in early interventions should always be voluntary. Affected individuals should never be subjected to coercion and certainly should not be required to participate in any mode of psychological intervention. Research suggests that the majority of individuals are able to cope appropriately with trauma without outside intervention, suggesting that perhaps simply supporting normal adaptive responses is an appropriate crisis response.

There is evidence that early, brief, and focused psychotherapeutic intervention can reduce distress in bereaved spouses, parents, and children. Cognitive behavioral approaches may help reduce incidence duration and severity of acute stress disorder, post-traumatic stress disorder, and depression in survivors. There are interventions (group and individual) that have not been proven effective and may do harm. Interventions that rely on detailed recall of traumatic experiences have a high potential for inadvertent harm. Responsible leaders should select professionals who have the high degree of training, expertise, accountability, and responsibility to organize and implement these interventions.

Early interventions should be planned appropriately and facilitated by personnel who are trained in crisis response. Facilitators should be educated in the following:

- The nature of traumatic stress reactions and normal reactions to trauma
- Symptoms and risk factors associated with more serious problems
- Adaptive coping behaviors for mastering the effects of mass violence and disasters
- Screening techniques for identifying at-risk and symptomatic individuals
- Services available in the aftermath of mass violence and disasters

Facilitators should have a sense of the typical timelines of crisis responses and crisis aftermath. They will need to distinguish appropriate interventions at critical stages. Table 10.1, adapted from the NIH Publication No. 02-5138, Appendix B (2002), identifies the typical phases of a crisis, adjustment goals, typical behaviors, and the roles of helpers and mental health professionals. It offers an excellent overview of specific needs and interventions in the various phases of recovery from a critical incident.

PREPLANNING AN APPROPRIATE RESPONSE

In *Coping with Crisis: Lessons Learned,* Poland and McCormick (2000) describe the need to have a crisis team with a prepared, organized response to effectively cope with crisis on a school-wide level. Drawing from direct experience with intervening in school crisis events, they discuss essential elements for providing an effective response, emphasizing the importance of planning for communication in the aftermath of a crisis.

As in many scenarios, open and effective communication is often the venue through which healing and recovery begin or further damage is done. It is vital to be equipped for disseminating notifications regarding sentinel events to parents and communities. How, where, and when notifications are given regarding a traumatic event can significantly affect the impact of that event. Often people remember the exact time and place where they were notified of a critical incident. It is helpful to bear in mind that the initial notification will possibly remain etched in the memories of those impacted by that event for many years to come.

Additionally, good, clear communication is vital to controlling rumors. Faculty members, families, and students alike are vulnerable to the inevitable speculation that follows in the aftermath of a crisis. It is important to plan for an effective way to disseminate the facts appropriately and to dispel potentially harmful misinformation.

It is important to mobilize crisis team members to include administrators, counseling staff, nursing staff, and other prepared professionals to provide an immediate response and a periodic reassessment of needs and to continually monitor the recovery of individuals and the school community.

The recovery of a school and individual students will largely depend on the timely and organized response of professionals informed in best

TABLE 10.1   GENERAL TIMING OF EARLY INTERVENTIONS

Phase	Impact (0-48 hrs.)	Rescue (0-1 week)	Recovery (1-4 weeks)	Return to Life (2 weeks to 2 years)
Goals	Survival, communication	Adjustment	Appraisal, planning	Reintegration
Behavior	Fight/flight, freeze, surrender, etc.	Resilience vs. exhaustion	Grief reappraisal, intrusive memories, narrative formation	Adjustment vs. phobias, PTSD, avoidance, depression, etc.
Role of All Helpers	Rescue, protect	Orient, provide for needs	Respond with sensitivity	Continue to offer assistance
Role of Mental Health Professionals	Basic Needs · Establish security · Provide orientation · Facilitate communication · Assess the environment for ongoing threat Psychological First Aid · Support for most distressed · Facilitate family reunion · Provide information · Protect survivors from further harm · Reduce physiological arousal	Needs Assessment · Assess recovery environment · Identify need for interventions · Identify high-risk individuals · Make referrals for clinical evaluations Outreach and Information · Contact and identify individuals who have not requested services	Monitor the Recovery Environment · Observe and listen to those most affected · Monitor the environment for toxins · Monitor past and ongoing threats · Monitor services that are being provided	Treatment Reduce or ameliorate symptoms or improve functioning by using: · Individual, family, and group psychotherapy · Pharmacotherapy · Short-term or long-term hospitalization

practices responses in the wake of a critical incident. In the school environment, counselors are often considered the experts in mental health concerns. It is therefore imperative that counselors be prepared. The school staff, students, and their families will likely look to the counselors for guidance.

GROUP PROCESSING OF CRITICAL INCIDENTS

Group processing of critical incidents, sometimes referred to as *critical incident debriefing,* refers to the verbal processing of the facts, personal experiences, and emotional reactions to a crisis. The intent of an after-incident group processing is to clarify the facts, share the experience, and ease the emotional volatility associated with the traumatic experience. It is very cathartic to know that you're not alone, that others share your perspective and pain. It's extremely helpful to break down barriers of isolation.

Based on the assumption that the discussion of a traumatic event soon after the event can reduce the potential for psychological harm, a variety of modalities have evolved recently. Many programs have grown up in response to a perceived need to provide such services for groups of individuals who have been directly or indirectly exposed to a traumatic event. It has sometimes been presumed that the failure to provide after-incident processing and/or counseling services can adversely affect psychological functioning.

Consider a student who is significantly distressed by the death of a very close classmate. Almost immediately, she begins to have chronic absences. Once an honor student, she soon begins to lose interest in her classes and subsequently experiences academic failure. Eventually, she decides to quit school. The initial incident has now caused the additional trauma of experiencing personal failure. Although this sample is fictional, research has demonstrated that the long-term effects of trauma can be very costly to the individual—often more devastating than the initial event.

However, results of research regarding the benefits of psychological debriefings or group processing of critical events have been mixed. Some studies have indicated there is potential for harm with certain types of interventions. Therefore, it is vital that when and if a psychological group processing is deemed appropriate, it be conducted by a trained facilitator, in accordance with the highest standards for best practice. Participation in any type of crisis intervention should be voluntary.

GUIDELINES FOR A GROUP PROCESSING

Goals

The primary goal of group processing is to provide information and to confront misinformation. We recommend that administrators, counseling staff, and other crisis team members first assemble with the faculty to discuss the critical incident and to announce plans for the school's response. In an elementary school setting, it would typically not be appropriate to plan for a school-wide meeting to provide notification and/or to process a critical incident. Often notifications of high-impact events (those that directly affect an individual student or student population, or incidents involving graphic or perpetrator-induced violence, death, or the potential for unresolved fear and anxiety) are left to parents, but sometimes it is deemed appropriate to meet with a class or in small-group settings to process a critical incident.

In a classroom setting, the teacher (or familiar authority figure with close rapport with students) should be present, along with a school counselor or mental health professional. The intent of the meeting should be discussed (to provide information, clarify facts, answer questions, and to discuss any reactions or concerns related to the incident).

A secondary goal of a group processing is to communicate a sense of security and preparedness to the students. Often the presence of an administrator to offer reassurances can be helpful. It is important to communicate that the school will get through this event and that return to normalcy is the expectation.

A third goal of group processing is to provide students with the opportunity to share their experiences and recognize that they are not alone in their thoughts and reactions. Recognizing that their reactions are normal and perhaps even typical can often alleviate further anxiety and lesson the impact of trauma.

Education regarding effective coping strategies for handling stress should be a fourth goal. This is an ideal time to provide general instruction in resuming normal routines, exercise, relaxation, and seeking emotional support from family, friends, school, and community.

The final goal of group processing might be to assess the need for additional services. As information is presented, events discussed, and feelings and reactions described, counselors and other mental health professionals can use this opportunity to recognize any maladaptive responses or high-risk students.

Considerations for Inclusion

When handled appropriately, group processing of critical incidents is likely to be beneficial for most individuals but not all. Individuals with a known mental or emotional disorder may not respond well to a group session. An individual's inappropriate response might negatively impact the entire group, potentially leading to the session becoming unduly stressful for all and possibly exacerbating the negative effects of the initial trauma rather than defusing them.

Group processing should typically involve individuals within a close range of physical and emotional relatedness to the critical incident. That is to say, direct victims should not be grouped with witnesses. Likewise, direct witnesses should not be grouped with secondary witnesses. For example, a group of students who witnessed a fatal injury during a playground accident will have distinct needs from those of students who heard about the incident later.

Attendance and discussion of a critical incident should always be voluntary. Some individuals have a rigid psychological defense system that allows them to cope with trauma by effectively avoiding remembrances of that event. Research indicates that forcing these individuals to discuss or confront a traumatic event may actually increase the likelihood of post-trauma symptoms. These individuals are best identified by self-report: When asked whether or not they would like to discuss a specified traumatic event, these individuals will answer negatively. In a school setting, it is imperative to invite students to participate, rather than coerce.

Format

Following is a general outline for conducting a group processing.

    I.   Describe the Facts of the Incident

        a. Provide accurate information regarding the critical incident

  b. Limit discussion to general facts, avoiding graphic descriptions

  c. Allow a question-and-answer session to clarify events

II. Discussion of Personal Experience

  a. Allow sharing of personal experiences

  b. Encourage acceptance of each individual's personal experience

III. Discussion of Feelings

  a. Allow participants to verbalize their feelings regarding the traumatic event

  b. Demonstrate acceptance and understanding for the range of emotional reactions

IV. Education on Symptoms of Stress and Grief Reactions (as relevant)

  a. Discuss normal and predictable stress symptoms related to traumatic events

  b. Discuss grief reactions and/or stages of grief

V. Suggestions of Coping Strategies or Stress-Reducing Behaviors

  a. Resuming normal routines

  b. Exercise

  c. Support resources available in school or community

For more specific training and guidelines, a wide variety of resources are available. For example, the International Critical Incident Stress Foundation, Inc. (ICISF), is an excellent resource dedicated to the prevention and mitigation of disabling stress. ICISF provides continuing education and training in emergency mental health services for mental health professionals and counselors, as well as consultation in the establishment of crisis and disaster response programs for varied organizations and communities worldwide.

Organizations offering continuing education for mental health professionals; national, state, and local mental health agencies; and most mental health and counseling professional organizations are also good resources for crisis response management. We strongly recommend that counselors and mental health professionals receive specific training in group processing of traumatic events prior to conducting any type of open processing of a high-impact incident.

*W*e found our school collaborations very rewarding and enjoyable. Most teachers, counselors, and school administrators were highly motivated to help children with emotional and behavioral problems. The problem was that they often felt at a loss as to how to begin. Brainstorming sessions with teachers, parents, and counselors were extremely helpful in delineating problems, precipitants, and identifying workable solutions. Additional factors essential for success were setting realistic goals, planning for contingencies, flexibility, a willingness to accept setbacks, and arranging for regular follow-up with the team until symptoms abated or were resolved.

In our experience, many school counselors needed only minimal consultation and guidance to get them off and running with interventions. Often, with a few ideas planted, more would sprout from teachers, parents, counselors, and even the children themselves, all of whom had previously felt at a loss. Many of the interventions gained momentum on their own and gave the counselors and teachers the launching pad and confidence to grow effective programs. It turned out that as long as it felt as though we were all working together and had some semblance of a plan, working with children with emotional and behavioral problems in the schools was great fun and quite gratifying indeed.

Techniques for Counseling Socially Impaired Children

HOW TO SHOW YOU ARE BEING A GOOD LISTENER

1. *Make eye contact.*

2. *Put down anything you're doing or looking at.*

3. *Don't talk while the other person is talking.*

4. *Respond to what the speaker says (e.g., answer a question).*

5. *Ask a relevant question or make a relevant comment.*

6. *Repeat back parts of what the speaker says.*

7. *Paraphrase what the speaker says.*

FEELINGS VOCABULARY CARDS

SAD	EXCITED	ECSTATIC
MAD	HAPPY	FURIOUS
DREAMY	DISAPPOINTED	TERRIFIED
HOPEFUL	FRUSTRATED	WORRIED
SCARED	EMBARRASSED	UPSET
IN LOVE	THOUGHTFUL	CONFUSED

THINGS THAT <u>DON'T</u> HELP A FRIEND WHO'S UPSET

1. **Vague Response**

   "I understand how you feel."

   This response is not specific enough. If you say this, you may seem insincere or patronizing. Use a specific feeling word.

2. **Invalidating Feelings**

   "That's no reason to be upset."

   It is important to emphasize with kids that all feelings are important to the person experiencing them. You can ask them whether the same things that make them sad or angry make their brother or mother or teacher sad or angry. You can help them recognize that we all react differently to the same situation. What makes other children sad or angry might not affect them the same way. The point to remember is that we all have had the same feelings at one time or other. We all know what it is like to feel angry, sad or disappointed. The message to share is that "I know what it's like to feel _____ (fill in the blank with a specific word)" or "I can see that you are feeling _____ (fill in)." Also, by conveying you understand their feelings and inviting them to talk, you are showing you think their feelings are important. This is a great gift to give a friend, and it's free.

3. **Problem Solving**

   "It will be easy to fix your bike," or "Why don't you just buy another one?"

   Many kids (and adults, for that matter) make this mistake when trying to comfort a friend. We think everything would be fine if we could just solve the problem. Problem solving is a useful skill, but the timing must be right. Initially, what is helpful when others are upset is simply expressing empathy, validating their feelings, and inviting them to talk about their feelings. Rushing to solve their problems often makes others feel as if their feelings are being dismissed or invalidated.

4. **Giving Advice**

   "Why don't you just go tell the teacher you didn't cheat?"

   Again, advice right off the bat is not usually helpful or welcomed by a friend who is hurting. Instead, wait for advice to be sought. In the meantime, express empathy and actively listen. Just be there.

THINGS THAT <u>DO</u> HELP A FRIEND WHO'S UPSET

1. **Reflective Listening**
   As mentioned, reflective listening is simply repeating back part of what someone says or paraphrasing it. It is very therapeutic and makes others feel as though you care and are listening.

2. **Empathy**
   This refers to trying to understand what someone is feeling and conveying it back to him or her.

   Formulas for Expressing Empathy

   You sound _____ (fill in with feeling word).

   You look _____ (fill in with feeling word).

   I sense that you feel _____ (fill in with feeling word).

3. **Collaborative Problem Solving**
   Greene (2001) has developed a program for explosive children built around an intervention he has termed *collaborative problem solving.* His program involves adults assisting children by essentially empowering them to solve their own problems. They do this by serving as a sounding board and providing some emotional support in the face of a crisis or conflict. This technique can also be a therapeutic intervention that friends use to support each other and can be taught to children 10 and over as an option for helping a friend in crisis. It is quite different than attempting to solve friends' problems for them when they are upset, which would likely leave them feeling inadequate and as if their feelings were dismissed.

4. **Just Being There / Just Listening**
   This is fairly self-explanatory. When people are upset, it is helpful just to be with them and listen if they want or need to talk. Having someone who cares about you standing by when you're upset is extremely healing. You don't have to say a word, *just be there.*

OPTIONS FOR APPROACHING
SOCIAL CONFLICT THAT WORK

1. *Compromise.*

2. *Use humor (i.e., make a joke to disarm).*

3. *Apologize.*

4. *Be assertive.*

5. *Ignore/walk away.*

6. *Take turns.*

7. *Use chance (e.g., flip a coin).*

SAMPLE SOCIAL CONFLICT SCENARIOS

Your best friend likes the same boy you do.	Your friend borrowed your bike and broke it.	Your mom said you have to clean your room but your friends are waiting for you outside to play.
You caught your friend cheating on a test.	You have invitations to two birthday parties on the same day.	You want to play soccer but your friend wants to play football.
One of your friends dislikes your other friend.	You failed a test.	You can't agree with your sister on what to watch on TV.
You lost your new jacket.	You can't find your homework.	Your teacher accused you of doing something you didn't do.
Your sister won't stop singing.	Your friend lied to you.	The boy next to you won't stop talking in class.

COMMUNICATION STYLES

Passive: A passive style of communication implies saying or doing nothing when faced with a social conflict or distressing situation.

Passive-Aggressive: Passive-aggressive communication refers to a style whereby people display hostility or aggression in a covert way. For example, they might deliberately lose or forget something or show up late to meet someone with whom they are angry.

Aggressive: Aggressive communication refers to physical or verbal aggression, whereby overt hostility is expressed in a way intended to deliberately hurt others.

Assertive: Assertive communication is considered the ideal style. It involves openly and honestly expressing one's feelings without using shame, blame, or put-downs and making simple and clear requests of others.

EXAMPLE OF FOUR STYLES OF COMMUNICATION

You are in a crowded movie theater and the guys behind you won't stop talking.

a. *You ignore them. (Passive)*

b. *You politely ask them to stop talking so you can enjoy the movie. (Assertive)*

c. *You start talking loudly, too, to annoy them. (Passive-aggressive)*

d. *You throw your popcorn and drinks at them. (Aggressive)*

SAMPLE SCENARIOS FOR PRACTICING ASSERTIVE COMMUNICATION

a. *The bike repair shop overcharged you $20 and did work you didn't request.*

b. *The cafeteria server gave you the wrong lunch.*

c. *Your sister won't stop teasing you about your freckles.*

d. *Your friend wants to borrow your new game, but you don't want him to.*

e. *A bully butted in line.*

f. *The teacher accuses you of cheating, but you didn't.*

g. *You want to play basketball, but your friend wants to play baseball.*

h. *Your friend wants to borrow your new toy, but you don't wish to share it.*

i. *The waitress brought you the wrong order.*

ASSERTIVENESS FORMULA

I FEEL _____ ("I" state-
ment, identify and explain your feelings)

WHEN YOU _____ (Point out
the behavior you don't like without insulting, attacking)

BECAUSE (optional) _____ (Help the
other person understand your viewpoint, put him or her
in your shoes)

I WOULD LIKE _____ (Make a
request)

IN RETURN/THEN (optional) _____ (Let the
other person know the positive consequences for both of
you if he or she complies with your request)

TEASE HANDLES

1. **Ignoring/Walking Away:** Self-explanatory.

2. **Fogging:** Agree with the tease or even expand on it (e.g., in response to a child calling another ugly, teasing victim says, "That's right, I am ugly. I also have a terrible personality"). A simple but effective example of fogging is to simply say, "So what?" or "Prove it!" in response to a tease or insult.

3. **Put Down the Tease:** Make fun of the tease but not the teaser (e.g., in response to an old tease, say, "I've been hearing that since I was in kindergarten!").

4. **Broken Record:** In response to teasing, repeat in calm, monotone manner, "I don't like you teasing me and I'm not going to say anything back."

5. **Tell an Adult:** Self-explanatory.

Techniques for Counseling Anxious Children

RELAXATION LOG

Name: _____

Dates	Number of Minutes of Relaxation Practice						
	Mon	Tues	Wed	Thurs	Fri	Sat	Sun

RELAXATION EXERCISES

Deep Breathing Script:

Okay, are you all comfortable and have enough space from your neighbor? Now I want you to put your hand on your bellies and close your eyes. We're going to clear our minds and just concentrate on our breathing. We're going to learn how to take abdominal breaths, which is how newborn infants breathe. I want you to breathe in through your noses and take deep breaths, down into your abdomens. As you breathe in, you should feel your hand rising and falling. I'd like you to hold each breath for four seconds and then breathe out slowly, making a "whooshing" sound. Turn your mind to your breathing and tune in to your body. Clear your mind of any thoughts or worries. Now let's begin:

Take a deep breath in through your nose, slowly, deeply, and hold it, 1, 2, 3, 4. Now exhale slowly: whoooooosh (do it with them). That's one. Now again, deep breath in, hold it, 1, 2, 3, 4, exhale slowly, whoooooosh. That's two. (Repeat this with them for 10 cycles.)

Progressive Muscle Relaxation Script:

Now I want you to squeeze your fists as tight as you can. Squeeze tight, hold it, 1, 2, tight, tighter, 3, 4, 5, 6, 7. Now release. Now tighten your biceps as much as you can by making a muscle with your arms. Hold it, 1, 2, tight, tight, tight, 3, 4, 5, 6, 7. Now release. Now tense your triceps by straightening your arms and locking your elbows. Hold it, tighter, 1, 2, 3, tighter still, hold it, 4, 5, 6, 7. Now release. Now tighten your neck muscles by arching your head down, trying to touch your chest with your nose. Hold it, 1, 2, 3, tighter, 4, 5, 6, 7. Now release. (You can have them arch their heads in each direction, front, back, left, and right because the neck particularly often carries a great deal of muscle tension). Now tense your shoulders by arching them back as if you were trying to touch them together. Arch them back, hard, hold it, tighter, 1, 2, 3, 4, 5, 6, 7. Now release. (You can repeat the tense-release of the shoulder blades because this is also often a problem area.) Now raise your shoulders up, as if you were going to touch your ears. Hold it, higher, 1, 2, 3, 4, 5, 6, 7. Now tighten your chest by taking in a deep breath and holding it, 1, 2, 3, 4, 5, 6, 7. Now release. Now tighten your belly muscles by sucking your tummy in. Suck in your tummies—that's it, hold, 1, 2, 3, 4, 5, 6, 7. Now release. Now tighten your bum. Squeeze those cheeks—hold it, squeeze, 1, 2, 3, 4, 5, 6, 7. Now release. Now tighten your thighs by straightening your legs out. Hold the tension in your legs, 1, 2, 3, 4, 5, 6, 7. Now release. Now curl your toes up, curl them as hard as you can—hold it, 1, 2, 3, 4, 5, 6, 7. Now release. Last one: Curl your toes down, into the floor—hold it, 1, 2, 3, 4, 5, 6, 7. Release.

Imagery Script:

I want you to close your eyes and get ready to use your very best imagination. I really want you to go with me to the place I'm going to describe. Use all your senses and try hard to imagine the sights, sounds, smells, textures, and feelings that go along with the story.

You are visiting your Grandma at her farm. You just finished eating a hearty, warm lunch of grilled cheese sandwiches and tomato soup. You know how Grandma always spoils you! Your belly is just-right full and you feel completely satisfied. You're lying in a bed of straw in the barn. Smell that crisp country air with the smell of fresh straw and horses. You can hear the chickens clucking around outside. You nuzzle into the bed of straw and the barn kittens come out to play. They climb all over you and kiss your face with their sandpaper tongues. They purr and meow and wrestle with each other. This is a moment of pure bliss. You are at peace and wish this moment would never end.

You and your dad are sitting in the boat, leaning back, holding your fishing poles. You are in your favorite spot on the lake where the big fish bite. The sun is warm on your head and back but not too warm. The smell of lake water and the trees along the shore mix with the musty, fishy odor of your dad's fishing hat, which he is letting you wear. You can hear the sparrows chirping nearby and occasionally a fish jumps up to say hello. Your dad is so proud of you—you caught your first fish! A big catfish! Dad says you can take it home and Mom will serve it for dinner. The boat sways a little as the wind picks up. You watch the ripples in the lake as they build and fade. It's hypnotic. You feel so proud and warm and lucky. Now this is the life!

TYPES OF COGNITIVE DISTORTIONS COMMONLY EXPERIENCED BY ANXIOUS CHILDREN

1. **Mindreading:** Assuming you know what someone is thinking without checking.

2. **Name-Calling:** Using derogatory or pejorative labels to describe self or others (e.g., "He's a jerk or a liar or a loser" or "I'm so stupid or lazy or foolish").

3. **Assuming the Worst:** Convincing yourself that only the worst possible outcome will happen, when, in reality, the worst outcome is usually very unlikely (e.g., assuming that your friend didn't return your call because she no longer wants to be your friend, when it turns out she's sick in bed).

4. **Overestimating the Chances of Something Bad:** Assuming that a bad outcome is more likely than it really is (e.g., assuming you are going to fail a test because you only studied three nights, instead of four, even though you always do well in school).

5. **Not Giving Yourself Enough Credit:** Assuming you can't handle things when you really can (e.g., assuming you'd be devastated and unable to cope if you failed a class).

6. **Seeing Things in Black and White:** Viewing things as either all bad or all good, when most things and people are usually a mix of bad and good (e.g., assuming someone is a "total jerk" because he failed to say hello one morning).

7. **Ignoring the Positive:** Focusing entirely on the negative aspect of a situation and ignoring all the positive aspects (e.g., ruminating about getting 2 questions wrong, instead of 98 right).

SOCRATIC QUESTIONS FOR CHALLENGING DISTORTED THOUGHTS IN ANXIOUS CHILDREN

1. *Has my fear come true before?*

2. *What is the chance of my thought coming true?*

3. *Are there any other ways this situation could turn out?*

4. *What's the worst that could happen?*

5. *How have I done in the past in similar situations?*

6. *Can I think of any ways to cope with this situation?*

7. *Am I underestimating my ability to deal with this situation?*

COPING STATEMENTS

"Although I am uncomfortable, I can handle it."

"Just breathe…"

"This will pass…"

"I have many ways to cope."

"I can get help if I need it."

"I am ready for a difficult situation."

"I know what to do."

"I have options."

SAMPLE WORRY GAME

Directions: Cut out cards and divide into 2 piles: Socratic questions and worries. Take turns picking up a worry and a question and respond to the question for that particular worry. Give tokens or points for effort.

What evidence is there for or against the worry?	Are there any other ways this situation could turn out?	What is the very worst that could happen? What is so bad about that? What would I do?
Has this worry come true or occurred before?	How have I done in the past in similar situations?	What is the chance my worry will come true?
I'll get stuck in a stairwell	I'll get a bad grade	I'll get stuck in an elevator
I might get hurt	I'll get in trouble	I'll get lost
My mom might get hurt	I might get beat up	I'll be embarrassed

Name: _____

THOUGHT RECORD

Situation	
Thoughts	
Feelings	
My Plan (use relaxation, challenge my thoughts, get a buddy, face the feared situation)	

DESENSITIZATION HIERARCHY

Step 1 _____

Step 2 _____

Step 3 _____

Step 4 _____

Step 5 _____

Step 6 _____

Step 7 _____

Step 8 _____

Techniques for
Counseling
Disruptive Children

D.I.R.T.: A PROBLEM-SOLVING PNEUMONIC

D is for DEFINE the problem: The first step with children who are upset is to help them talk out their feelings and cool down. Sometimes it's helpful to assist them in performing relaxation exercises. The goal is to help them arrive at a point where the intensity of the feelings is no longer overwhelming and they feel back in control. As their arousal is lowered and their brains begin to reason, help them define the problem as specifically as possible.

I is for IDENTIFY choices: When children are ready, encourage them to use their "good brains" to identify options for approaching the problem. During the brainstorming, it's helpful if the counselor writes down the child's ideas. This exercise of writing down their thoughts gives validity and weight to their ideas. Children should be encouraged to develop as comprehensive a list as possible and not reject or withhold any ideas initially. The counselor may contribute some ideas, too, but should be careful not to be overbearing or critical of any of the initial suggestions.

R is for REFLECT on the choices: The next step would be to have children work through the list mentally, visualizing the likely outcome of each approach. After they have covered the list, they should be encouraged to pick the option that they think will result in the best outcome.

T is for TRY it out: Finally, encourage them to try out their chosen option and report back to you regarding the results.

SAMPLE PROBLEMS

The class bully was making fun of my best friend.	Another child stole my Game Boy.	My sister broke my Xbox.
I was accused of cheating, but I didn't.	My mother is always late to pick me up.	My friend told the whole school a secret of mine.
Another child stole my money.	Another child pushed me.	Another child butted in line.
I miss my best friend who moved away.	I can't find my homework.	I can't find my sneakers and the bus is here.
I wish I were better at soccer.	I borrowed my mom's sweater and lost it.	I think my teacher is mean.

REACTION CARDS

hotheaded	hotheaded	hotheaded
coolheaded	coolheaded	coolheaded

CONSEQUENCE CARDS

long-term	long-term	long-term
short-term	short-term	short-term

Sample Behavioral Contracts

SAMPLE BEHAVIORAL CONTRACT
FOR HOME AND SCHOOL

_____'s Behavioral Contract

Targets: 1. "I will speak only when it's my turn."
2. "I will follow directions by the count of 5."
3. "I will keep my hands and feet to myself."

Tracking: I will receive 1 point per target met at 10 a.m., 12 noon, and 2 p.m., for a possible total of 9 points per day.

My teacher will log the points into my log book and initial them 3 times per day.

I will review the log book with my parents each evening and they will also track my points.

Rewards Menu: 50 Points = Get to order pizza for dinner
100 Points = Trip to bowling alley with Dad
150 Points = Game for Nintendo

CALENDAR FOR TRACKING POINTS OR STICKERS

WEEK OF _____

		MON.	TUES.	WED.	THURS.	FRI.
a.m.	Target 1					
	Target 2					
	Target 3					
noon	Target 1					
	Target 2					
	Target 3					
p.m.	Target 1					
	Target 2					
	Target 3					

BEHAVIORAL CONTRACT FOR THE HOMEWORK/SCHOOLWORK–NEGLIGENT CHILD

_____'s Behavioral Contract

Targets

- Complete and turn in homework daily.
- Complete and turn in classwork daily.
- Attend all classes unless medically excused.

Tracking System

- _____must obtain signatures on day planner from all teachers whose classes were attended that day to verify classwork and homework completion and on-time submission. Teachers refuse to sign if homework or classwork not completed or turned in.
- _____must provide parent(s) with class schedule so signatures of appropriate teachers can be verified.
- Day planner with signatures shown to parent(s) daily.

Reward System

- For each day student meets all three targets, may have usual privileges (e.g., TV, time with friends, playing outside).
- When reaches 30 days of compliance, may earn special outing (e.g., zoo, bowling, movies, _____).
- Each day fails to meet targets, confined to room, usual privileges revoked.

Signatures:

Parent _____

Student _____

Teacher _____

BEHAVIORAL CONTRACT FOR A SELECTIVELY MUTE CHILD

_____'s Behavioral Contract

Target Behaviors

- "I will speak to my friends at recess."
- "I will speak to my parents on the phone in the classroom."
- "I will use words to communicate at the youth center." (Other targets could be used such as, "I will mouth the words I'd like to say," "I will speak to my teacher in a whisper," and later, "I will speak to my teacher loud enough to be heard two feet away," and so on.) No more than three targets should be attempted at once.

Special Arrangements

- The mother or father will call each day at _____ on the classroom phone.
- After first week, teacher assigns _____ a buddy for recess to count words.
- Classmates and youth center workers are aware of the program.

Tracking

- _____ receives one point per word spoken at recess or on the phone with parents in the classroom or spoken at any time to any peer/teacher/daycare provider on school grounds or at the youth center.
- An outgoing buddy will be appointed each day by the teacher to count words spoken at recess.
- The teacher will write the number of words/points earned on the chalkboard at the end of recess each day and record it on a card to be sent home.
- The youth center workers will write the number of words/points on a card each day.
- _____'s parents will give one penny for each point earned.

Rewards/Consequences

- Parents will not continue phone calls to classroom if _____ fails to speak at all on phone in classroom when they call at designated time.
- After 50 points are earned, the class has a party (movie, popcorn, the works!).
- Rewards Menu (provided at home by parents):

    Small—20 Points/Pennies (e.g., small toy, pizza, ice cream):

    _____

    Medium—40 Points/Pennies (e.g., bowling, movies, dinner out): _____

    Large—60 Points/Pennies (e.g., zoo, theme park, Xbox):

    _____

Achenbach, T. M., & Edelbrock, C. S. (1991). *Manual for the child behavior checklist and child behavior profile*. Burlington, VT: University of Vermont Department of Psychiatry.

Adler, A. (1933). First childhood recollection. *International Journal of Individual Psychology, 11,* 81–90.

Barkley, R. (1997). *The defiant child: A clinician's manual for assessment and parent training*. New York: Guilford Press.

Bar-On, R. (1997). *Bar-On emotional quotient inventory: User's manual*. Toronto: Multi-Health Systems, Inc.

Bernstein, G., Borchardt, C., & Perwien, A. (1996). Anxiety disorders in children and adolescents: A review of the past 10 years. *Journal of the American Academy of Child and Adolescent Psychiatry, 35,* 1110–1119.

Birmaher, B., Ryan, N., Williamson, D., Brent, D., & Kaufman, J.. (1996a). Childhood and adolescent depression: A review of the past 10 years. Part I. *Journal of the American Academy of Child and Adolescent Psychiatry, 35 (11),* 1427–1439.

Birmaher, B., Ryan, N., Williamson, D., Brent, D., & Kaufman, J. (1996b). Childhood and adolescent depression: A review of the past 10 years. Part II. *Journal of the American Academy of Child and Adolescent Psychiatry, 35 (12),* 1575–1583.

Bourne, E. (1995). *The anxiety and phobia workbook*. Oakland, CA: New Harbinger Publications.

Bowlby, J. (1979). *The making and breaking of affectional bonds*. London: Tavistock Publications.

Brooks, R., & Goldstein, S. (2001). *Raising resilient children*. Lincolnwood, IL: Contemporary Books.

Burns, David D. (1999). *The feeling good handbook*. New York: Penguin Group.

Cantwell, D. (1996). Attention deficit disorder: A review of the past 10 years. *Journal of the American Academy of Child and Adolescent Psychiatry, 35 (8):* 978–987.

Chamberlain, P., & Mihalic, S. F. (1998). Multidimensional treatment foster care. In D. S. Elliott (Series Ed.), *Book eight: Blueprints for violence prevention*. Boulder, CO: Institute of Behavioral Science, University of Colorado at Boulder.

163

Conners, C. K. (1997). *Conners' rating scales: Instruments for use with children and adolescents* (Rev. ed.). New York: Multi-Health Systems, Inc.

Faber, A., & Mazlish, E. (1980). *How to talk so kids will listen and listen so kids will talk.* New York: Avon Books.

Flannery-Schroeder, E., & Kendall, P. (1996). *Cognitive behavioral therapy for anxious children: Therapist manual for group treatment.* Ardmore, PA: Workbook Publishing.

Gordon, T. (2000). *Parent effectiveness training.* New York: Three Rivers Press.

Greene, R. (2001). *The explosive child.* New York: HarperCollins Publishers, Inc.

Hermes, S. (1998). *Assertiveness.* Center City, MN: Hazelden.

Kearney, C., & Albano, A. (2000). *When children refuse school.* San Antonio, TX: The Psychological Corporation.

Kendall, P. (2000). *Cognitive-behavioral therapy for anxious children: Therapist manual.* Ardmore, PA: Workbook Publishing.

Kovacs, M. (1985). The children's depression inventory (CDI). *Psychopharmocology Bulletin, 21,* 995–1124.

March, J. S., Parker, J. D., Sullivan, K., Stallings, P., & Conners, C. K. (1997). The multidimensional anxiety scale for children (MASC): Factor structure, reliability, and validity. *Journal of the American Academy of Child and Adolescent Psychiatry, 36*(4), 554–565.

Nelson, J. (1987). *Positive discipline.* New York: Ballantine Books.

National Institute of Mental Health (2002). *Mental health and mass violence: Evidence based early psychological intervention for victims/survivors of mass violence. A workshop to reach consensus on best practices.* NIH Publication No. 02-5138. Washington, DC: U.S. Government Printing Office.

Poland, S., & McCormick, J.S. (2000). *Coping with crisis: Lessons learned: A resource for schools, parents, and communities.* Longmont, CO: Sopris West.

Reynolds, C. R., & Richmond, B. O. (1978). What I think and feel: A revised measure of children's manifest anxiety. *Journal of Abnormal Psychology, 6*(2), 271–280.

Schaffer, D., & Pfeffer, C. (2001). Practice parameters for the assessment and treatment of children and adolescents with suicidal behavior. *Journal of the American Academy of Child and Adolescent Psychiatry, 40 (7)*: 24S–51S.

Shapiro, L. (1994). *The anger control tool kit.* Plainview, NY: Childswork/Childsplay.

Stein, H. (1993). *Adlerian client questionnaire.* San Francisco: Alfred Adler Institute of San Francisco.

U.S. Public Health Service (2000). *Report of the surgeon general's conference on children's mental health: A national action agenda.* Washington, D.C.: Department of Health and Human Services.